On

Sale, Securities, and Insurance

Sources in Early Modern Economics, Ethics, and Law

General Editors

The disciplines of economics, ethics, and law cannot be detached from a historical background that was, it is increasingly recognized, religious in nature. Economists Adam Smith and Léon Walras drew on the work of sixteenth- and seventeenth-century Spanish theologians who strove to understand the process of exchange and trade in order to better articulate subjective value, a dynamic theory of money, the role of the merchant, and the concept of marginal utility. Likewise, political theorists John Neville Figgis and Otto von Gierke drew on the work of sixteenth- and seventeenth-century Dutch, Swiss, German, and Spanish jurists and ethicists who articulated concepts that laid the foundation for federalist political structures, constitutionalism, popular sovereignty, natural-law jurisprudence, and limited government in the Western legal tradition. After a long period in which economics, ethics, and law became detached from theology, many economists, legal scholars, political theorists, and theologians now see the benefit of studying early modern economic, ethical, and legal texts in their full cultural, often religious, context. This series, *Sources in Early Modern Economics, Ethics, and Law*, provides first-ever English translations and editions of some of the most formative but previously inaccessible texts that shaped the disciplines of economics, ethics, and law in the early modern era and beyond. These inexpensive translations of seminal texts will make substantive contributions to contemporary interdisciplinary discussion.

Editorial Board

On

Sale, Securities, and Insurance

Leonardus Lessius

Translated by Wim Decock and Nicholas De Sutter

Introduction by Wim Decock

CLP Academic
Grand Rapids · Michigan

Refo500

On Sale, Securities, and Insurance

Translated by Wim Decock and Nicholas De Sutter

Cover image: Castle Arenberg, part of the Katholieke Universiteit Leuven, Belgium
License: Wikimedia Commons
Photo credit: Juhanson
URL: https://commons.wikimedia.org/wiki/File:Castle_Arenberg,_Katholieke_Universiteit_Leuven_adj.jpg
Inset photo: Österreichische Nationalbibliothek, Wien. Image ID: PORT_00108664_01 (Lessius Leonard) (http://www.bildarchivaustria.at/Pages/ImageDetail.aspx?p_iBildID=8097588). Used by permission.

ISBN: 978-1-938948-11-4

CHRISTIAN'S LIBRARY PRESS

An imprint of the Acton Institute
for the Study of Religion & Liberty

98 E. Fulton
Grand Rapids, Michigan 49503
Phone: 616.454.3080
Fax: 616.454.9454
www.clpress.com

Interior composition by Judy Schafer
Cover design by Peter Ho
Editorial management by Andrew M. McGinnis

Printed in the United States of America

Contents

Sources in Early Modern Economics, Ethics, and Law

Series Introduction

Jordan J. Ballor
Stephen J. Grabill

For the same underlying reasons that moral theology is held in disrepute by many Western intellectuals, modern economists tend to glibly dismiss or even simply ignore the economic ideas of the scholastics, whether those of the twelfth or the seventeenth century. For many intellectuals nowadays, moral theology has come to signify a passé form of religious thinking that embraces irrationality and dogmatism, and economic historians—along with notable astrophysicists, geneticists, paleontologists, political analysts, philosophers, and ethicists—have all espoused this line of thought. Among the latter, in particular, the identification of scholastic economics (or the "canonical concept of market behavior," as it is sometimes called) with Aristotelian metaphysics and ecclesiastical authority has made modern economic professionals reticent or, at the very least unreceptive, to acknowledging any sophisticated analytical contribution to monetary and value theory by the Schoolmen or the Doctors—their sixteenth- and seventeenth-century heirs.

The severing of economic ideas from their original historical and metaphysical contexts becomes especially pronounced in the contemporary debate over the prehistory of economics. Invariably, most mainstream economic historians locate the birth of modern economics in Adam Smith, the mercantilists, and the physiocrats. For historian of economics Mark Blaug, the prehistory of economics begins with the seventeenth-century mercantilists and not, as the revisionists insist, with either the ancient Greeks or the medieval scholastics. He coins the term *pre-Adamite economics* to methodologically define and restrict the era of prehistory to Smith's immediate and direct historical precursors: the seventeenth-century mercantilists, the physiocrats, and the British free-trade writers of the eighteenth century.

The broader question of whether the prehistory of economics should start in the thirteenth century or much earlier is, in Blaug's estimation, "an afterthought."[1] An afterthought, we might infer, which could presumably surface information that would challenge positivist assumptions about human behavior and social cohesion and one that will yield few, if any, new insights into quantitative methods and models. Where the scholastics analyzed economic and commercial transactions as either ethical or legal matters involving the application of natural law to civil contracts, "it was the mercantilists," contends Blaug, "who, long before Adam Smith, broke with the canonical conception of market behavior as a moral problem and fashioned the concept of 'economic man.'" These mercantilists

> believed in the direct power of self-interest and in matters of domestic economic policy came near to advocating laissez-faire. Adam Smith was not the first to have confidence in the workings of the 'invisible hand.' Nor is it necessary to

1. Mark Blaug, *Economic Theory in Retrospect*, 5th ed. (Cambridge: Cambridge University Press, 1997), 29.

> appeal to scholastic influences to account for his grasp of the determination of prices by demand and supply.[2]

Regardless of whether it is necessary to appeal to scholastic influences to explain how Smith, in particular, understood price and value to be determined, such a determination does not speak to the wider issue of whether such seminal figures in the history of economics as Bernardo Davanzati (1529–1606), Hugo Grotius (1583–1645), Samuel von Pufendorf (1632–1694), Gershom Carmichael (1672–1729), Francis Hutcheson (1694–1746), Jean-Jacques Burlamaqui (1694–1748), Adam Ferguson (1723–1816), Ferdinando Galiani (1728–1787), Auguste Walras (1801–1866), and Léon Walras (1834–1910) were influenced by scholastic treatments of price and value. Neither does this judgment determine, for that matter, whether Smith's entire system of thought remains intelligible if the role he assigns to teleology, final causes, divine design, and virtue is disregarded as merely ornamental.[3] In this wider respect, therefore, the modern quibble over scholastic influences in Smith is a red herring because, as Langholm attests, it sidesteps serious historical investigation into the continuities and discontinuities between scholastic and modern economic ideas.[4] Furthermore, it also has the convenient side effect of

2. Blaug, *Economic Theory in Retrospect*, 31.

3. See James E. Alvey, "The Secret, Natural Theological Foundation of Adam Smith's Work," *Journal of Markets & Morality* 7, no. 2 (Fall 2004): 335–61. See also Paul Oslington, ed., *Adam Smith as Theologian* (New York: Routledge, 2011).

4. "From an analytical and terminological point of view," writes Langholm, "there is much of scholastic teaching that can be seen to have survived into modern economics. This is not surprising, since (at least if this observation is limited to our Western civilization) it was in the high Middle Ages that the foundations were laid for the kind of systematic reasoning about social relationships that has run on continually to the present day. Sometimes, as in the case of the fairness of the market price, it was deemed pertinent above to point out a subtle shift in the moral basis that supported an apparently unaltered doctrine. Elsewhere, where doctrines

downplaying the importance of teleology and natural theology in the thought of Smith himself and other seventeenth-, eighteenth-, and nineteenth-century political economists.

By methodologically constricting the prehistory of economics to the mercantilists and the physiocrats, as positivist historiographers commend, economic history congeals around such characteristically "modern" concerns as the concept of "economic man," self-interest, and the emancipation of economics from the so-called canonical concept of market behavior. This arbitrary limitation of which ideas and which people carry weight in economic history only serves to bolster twentieth-century positivist assumptions, particularly those of value neutrality and *homo economicus*, the assumption that humans act as rational and self-interested agents who desire wealth, avoid unnecessary labor, and seek to order their decision making exclusively around those goals. In the end, the modern reduction of the prehistory of economics to the seventeenth-century mercantilists can be put in the form of an Occam's razor-like question: Why appeal to scholastic influences to illumine modern notions of money,

---

have changed as radically as in the case of lending at interest, the scholastics can still be credited with posing the terms of an ongoing argument. Therefore, it would seem that much of the old vessel remained to receive new content. The question is how completely it was ever emptied of the ferment prepared for it in the medieval schools. This subject requires a book rather than a few lines. In fact, it has been the subject of many books, some of them provoked or inspired by Max Weber's ideas about religion and capitalism. For simplicity, let us recall that scholastic economics rested on three intellectual traditions. The first support was the tradition of the Bible and the Church Fathers with its emphasis on individual duty. The second was the tradition of the recently rediscovered Roman law with its emphasis on individual rights. The two traditions were made to balance briefly and precariously in the Thomist synthesis by means of a third support in Aristotelian social philosophy." See Odd Langholm, "Scholastic Economics," in *Pre-Classical Economic Thought: From the Greeks to the Scottish Enlightenment*, ed. S. Todd Lowry (Boston/Dordrecht/Lancaster: Kluwer Academic Publishers, 1987), 132–33.

value, and price when all the basic elements of classical economics are already embedded in mercantilism?

The most straightforward reply is that seminal ideas, which include revolutionary economic ideas, never develop in intellectual, historical, religious, philosophical, or geographical vacuums. "Enlightened," secular reaction to the medieval Church's temporal jurisdiction and to theology's intellectual hegemony as the queen of the sciences has created a modern milieu in which scholars are no longer even aware of the historical influence that fundamental Christian doctrines have exerted in Western culture and university life.[5] From very early times, Christian theologians assumed that the application of patterns of discursive reasoning (as in the scholastic method, which was a method instituted by medieval Christian theologians and adapted and applied for subsequent centuries) could yield an increasingly accurate understanding not only of God's word and moral will but also of the created order itself.

Thus the systematic application of reason to a variety of intellectual undertakings, including economic problems, was not the invention of the Enlightenment. Rather, the application of reason within a coherent intellectual framework is the legacy of Christian scholasticism—the method of the medieval and early modern schools. The application of this scholastic method led to increased understanding of the world and human affairs, and spurred efforts to formulate logical explanations of regular occurrences in nature. "All things possess order amongst themselves: this order is the form that makes the world resemble God," wrote Dante in the *Divine Comedy*.[6] It can be argued that the specific application of scholastic method to economic

5. See Chris L. Firestone and Nathan Jacobs, eds., *The Persistence of the Sacred in Modern Thought* (Notre Dame: University of Notre Dame Press, 2012).

6. Dante, *Paradise*, trans. Anthony Esolen (New York: Modern Library, 2004), 1:103–5, p. 9.

problems became the seedbed for innovative ideas that, after much dialectical refinement, came to shape the world of modern economics. The truth of this statement does not rest on modernity's own understanding of its birth, development, or future trajectory but rather on the demonstrable "internal interconnections and affinities among ideas, their dynamism or 'particular go' (Lovejoy's phrase), and the logical pressures they are capable of exerting on the minds of those that think them."[7]

Assent to this claim, however, will require the positivist historian to reconsider not only the relationship between metaphysical schemata and intellectual traditions, which, in turn, will require an acknowledgement of the indispensable role of theological doctrines in the history of ideas,[8] but it will also require an admission that the recent detachment of economics from morality is itself a novelty, an aberration from a long-standing tradition within political economy itself.[9] In Alvey's judgment,

---

7. Francis Oakley, *Natural Law, Laws of Nature, Natural Rights: Continuity and Discontinuity in the History of Ideas* (New York and London: Continuum, 2005), 9.

8. See Oakley, *Natural Law, Laws of Nature, Natural Rights*, 13–34. See also the various essays in Oakley's *Politics and Eternity: Studies in the History of Medieval and Early-Modern Political Thought* (Leiden: Brill, 1999); Oakley, *Omnipotence, Covenant, and Order: An Excursion in the History of Ideas from Abelard to Leibniz* (Ithaca: Cornell University Press, 1984); Oakley, *Kingship: The Politics of Enchantment* (Oxford: Blackwell Publishing, 2006); and William J. Courtenay, *Covenant and Causality in Medieval Thought: Studies in Philosophy, Theology, and Economic Practice* (London: Variorum Reprints, 1984).

9. Broadly, on the historical constriction and positivism of contemporary economic thinking, see John D. Mueller, *Redeeming Economics: Rediscovering the Missing Element* (Wilmington, DE: ISI Books, 2010). See also Jeffrey T. Young, *Economics as a Moral Science: The Political Economy of Adam Smith* (Cheltenham, UK: Edward Elgar, 1997); James Alvey, "A Short History of Economics as a Moral Science," *Journal of Markets & Morality* 2, no. 1 (Spring 1999): 53–73; Ricardo F. Crespo, "Is Economics a Moral Science?," *Journal of Markets & Morality* 1, no. 2 (Fall 1998): 201–11; Peter J.

> There are two major reasons why economics has become detached from moral concerns. First, the natural sciences came to be seen as successful, and the attempt was made to emulate that success in economics by applying natural science methods, including mathematics, to economic phenomena. Second, the self-styled economic science came to adopt positivism, which ruled out moral issues from science itself.[10]

It is the latter recognition, perhaps more than any other, that squares the revisionists off against the positivists in the debate over the prehistory of economics.

When the positivistic bias begins to be put aside and we look anew at works from earlier periods, we find the early modern era to be a rich source of intellectual ferment on economic, ethical, and legal and political topics. In the sixteenth and early seventeenth centuries, a small but influential group of theologians and jurists centered in Spain attempted to synthesize the Roman legal texts with Aristotelian and Thomistic moral philosophy. The movement began with the revival of Thomistic philosophy in Paris, where, as Camacho recounts, "Pierre Crockaert underwent an intellectual conversion from nominalist philosophy to the philosophy of Thomas Aquinas."[11]

Shortly before 1225, the year of Aquinas' birth, Aristotle's works on metaphysics, physics, politics, and ethics became available in

Boettke, "Is Economics a Moral Science? A Response to Ricardo F. Crespo," *Journal of Markets & Morality* 1, no. 2 (Fall 1998): 212–19; and Crespo, "Is Economics a Moral Science? A Response to Peter J. Boettke," *Journal of Markets & Morality* 1, no. 2 (Fall 1998): 220–25; Jeffrey T. Young, *Economics as a Moral Science: The Political Economy of Adam Smith* (Cheltenham, UK: Edward Elgar, 1997).

10. Alvey, "A Short History of Economics as a Moral Science," 53.

11. Francisco Gómez Camacho, "Later Scholastics: Spanish Economic Thought in the Sixteenth and Seventeenth Centuries," in *Ancient and Medieval Economic Ideas and Concepts of Social Justice*, ed. S. Todd Lowry and Barry Gordon (Leiden and New York: Brill, 1998), 503.

the West, and, within the span of a generation, Aristotelianism, which had been brought to Europe by Arabic scholars, would be a serious contender in medieval thought. Thomas sought a rapprochement between the Greek philosophical tradition that Aristotle represented and the Christian divine ideas tradition articulated by the likes of Augustine, pseudo-Dionysius, and Bonaventure. In 1512, Crockaert published his commentary on the last part of Thomas' *Summa theologicae* with the help of a student, Francisco de Vitoria (ca. 1483–1546).[12]

Approximately two hundred years before Thomas was born, the *Corpus iuris civilis* of Justinian had been rediscovered and had become the object of academic disputation. However, the traditions of Roman law and Aristotelian and Thomistic philosophy existed in relative isolation from one other, at least until the early sixteenth century in Spain. "In the sixteenth and early seventeenth centuries," states Camacho, "a synthesis was finally achieved by that group of theologians and jurists known to historians of law as the 'late scholastics' or the 'Spanish natural law school.'"[13] Schumpeter concurs with this judgment and adds, "It is within their systems of moral theology and law that economics gained definite if not separate existence, and it is they who come nearer than does any other group to having been the 'founders' of scientific economics."[14] The Salamancans in particular, writes Moss,

12. Camacho, "Later Scholastics: Spanish Economic Thought in the Sixteenth and Seventeenth Centuries," 503.

13. Camacho, "Later Scholastics: Spanish Economic Thought in the Sixteenth and Seventeenth Centuries," 503.

14. Joseph Schumpeter, *History of Economic Analysis*, ed. Elizabeth Booty Schumpeter (Oxford: Oxford University Press, 1954), 97: "And not only that it will appear, even, that the bases they laid for a serviceable and well-integrated body of analytic tools and propositions were sounder than was much subsequent work, in the sense that a considerable part of the economics of the later nineteenth century might have been developed from those bases more quickly and with less trouble than it actually cost

> were as interested in a general theory of how exchange rates between different currencies are formed as in explaining why a bill of exchange is worth more in one region of Spain than in another region. Was the agio or exchange premium evidence of usury and therefore immoral behavior on the part of merchants and traders, or rather something 'natural' governed by the basic laws of supply and demand?[15]

The case of this so-called School of Salamanca is just one example of the rich intellectual traditions that have far too often been ignored or downplayed by contemporary scholarship. The coherent intellectual framework of Christian scholasticism reverberates not only in the field of economics but also in the related areas of ethics and law. Thus, political theorists John Neville Figgis and Otto von Gierke drew on the work of a variety of sixteenth- and seventeenth-century Dutch, Swiss, German, and Spanish jurists and ethicists who articulated concepts that laid the foundation for federalist political structures, constitutionalism, popular sovereignty, natural-law jurisprudence, and limited government in the Western legal tradition.[16] The diversity and variety of relevant sources from this period is underscored by the contribution of Protestant scholars, who produced significant scholastic works as well as more occasional treatises. Much of the early Protestant thought on economics, ethics, and law attaches to their homiletical and exegetical work in addition to the achieve-

---

to develop it, and that some of that subsequent work was therefore in the nature of a time- and labor-consuming detour."

15. Laurence S. Moss, "Introduction," in *Economic Thought in Spain: Selected Essays of Marjorie Grice-Hutchinson*, ed. Laurence S. Moss and Christopher K. Ryan (Brookfield, VT: Edward Elgar, 1993), xv.

16. On Johannes Althusius in particular, see Otto von Gierke, *The Development of Political Theory*, trans. Bernard Freyd (New York: Howard Fertig, 1966), 70; and John Neville Figgis, *Studies of Political Thought: From Gerson to Grotius, 1414–1625* (Cambridge: Cambridge University Press, 1907), 175–85.

ments in systems of moral theology and philosophy. The Dutch Reformed legal thinker Johannes Althusius (1563–1638) stands as a representative example in this regard, and his contributions to the development of Western legal and political traditions are becoming increasingly appreciated.[17] After a long period in which economics, ethics, and law became detached from theology, many economists, legal scholars, political theorists, and theologians now see the benefit of studying early modern economic, ethical, and legal texts in their full cultural, often religious, context.

The Sources in Early Modern Economics, Ethics, and Law series is the latest installment in the excavation of the mines of early modern theological thought on these topics. The aim of this series is to offer economists, intellectual historians, moral theologians, and graduate students in the fields of economics, economic ethics, economic history, banking history, political economy, and moral theology a useful and accessible collection of some of the most important early modern texts in the fields of economics, ethics, and law. Now, for the first time, the unabridged texts of works such as Martín de Azpilcueta's *Commentary on the Resolution of Money* (1556), Luis de Molina's *Treatise on Money* (1597), and Juan de Mariana's *Treatise on the Alteration of Money* (1609), as well as selections from larger works such as Johannes Althusius' *Dicaeologicae* (1617) and Girolamo Zanchi's *Omnium operum theologicorum* (1619) will be available as stand-alone volumes in English translation and in modern editions with scholarly annotations. We hope that the publication of these primary texts in a series of paperbacks will help to facilitate

17. See, for instance, John Witte Jr., "A Demonstrative Theory of Natural Law: The Original Contribution of Johannes Althusius," in *Public Theology for a Global Society: Essays in Honor of Max L. Stackhouse*, ed. Deirdre King Hainsworth and Scott R. Paeth (Grand Rapids: Eerdmans, 2010), 21–36; and Thomas O. Hueglin, *Early Modern Concepts for a Late Medieval World: Althusius on Community and Federalism* (Waterloo, ON: Wilfrid Laurier University Press, 1999).

exploration of the continuities and discontinuities, agreements and disagreements, innovations and ruptures among theological communities during the latter half of the sixteenth and the early seventeenth century.

The translations and modern editions (in conjunction with the introductions by leading authorities) will show the sophistication with which Christian thinkers from a variety of confessional and theological perspectives examined issues such as the role and responsibilities of the civil magistrates, the existence and efficacy of natural law, usury, and the ethics of moneylending, as well as the new process of using bills of exchange (*cambium per litteras*) to replace the cumbersome and dangerous transportation of metallic coins between commercial fairs, which led not only to new scholastic insights on interest, credit, and international trade but also to a much more comprehensive analysis of monetary exchange and banking practices than had been undertaken before. The texts will also address the questions as particular as why the same currency was worth more in one region than another area's currency, and, moreover, why the rate of exchange fluctuated between one area and the next. These moral and economic concerns, along with many others, will be addressed in detail throughout the course of the series by some of the leading, and heretofore underappreciated, authorities from the early modern era.

Abbreviations

Cod.	Corpus Iuris Civilis, Codex
Dig.	Corpus Iuris Civilis, Digesta
Inst.	Corpus Iuris Civilis, Institutiones
Auth.	Corpus Iuris Civilis, Novellarum Justiniani collectio authentica
Dec. Grat.	Corpus Iuris Canonici, Decretum Gratiani
Dec. Greg.	Corpus Iuris Canonici, Decretales Gregorii IX
Liber Sextus	Corpus Iuris Canonici, Decretales Bonifatii VIII

INTRODUCTION*

Wim Decock

The intimate connection between economics, ethics, and law can hardly be expressed any better than by the following late medieval image of the spiritual journey to God:

> We are like a merchant on his way to the market, carrying with him a bag full of gold money with which to buy splendid and expensive goods. Yet, out of the blue, a thief turns up and snatches away his purse. The merchant is left desperate. The human condition is the same. The money with which God has endowed us are the virtues: they enable us to buy eternal life. But then, all of a sudden, the devil appears. He tears apart our heart and the precious coin of virtue is stolen away. We are left outside of paradise.[1]

---

* The author wants to express his gratitude to the German Research Foundation (DFG), since part of the research necessary for the translation work was funded through the Heinz Maier-Leibnitz-Prize, awarded to Wim Decock in 2014.

1. This is a free adaptation of the metaphor developed by Thomas de Chobham (ca. 1160–ca. 1236) in his *Summa de arte praedicandi*, 6.2.373–82. Cf. O. I. Langholm, *The Merchant in the Confessional: Trade and Price in the Pre-Reformation Penitential Handbooks* (Leiden: Brill, 2003), 4–5.

This metaphor highlights the analogy between the risks of entrepreneurship and the perils threatening the salvation of the soul. It also throws light on the enterprise many scholars in sixteenth- and seventeenth-century scholasticism undertook to approach the rise of commercial capitalism from the perspective of justice. Dozens of treatises *On Justice and Right* (*De iustitia et iure*), *On Laws* (*De legibus*), and *On Restitution* (*De restitutione*) ensued from this undertaking.[2] A particularly influential masterpiece within this tradition was delivered in 1605 by Leonardus Lessius (1554–1623), a Jesuit moral theologian living in the Spanish-ruled Southern Netherlands. Lessius analyzed the market and tried to relieve merchants from their qualms of conscience by meticulously determining their rights and duties as a matter of justice.

Lessius' seminal contribution to early modern economics, ethics, and law transpires through his chapters on sale-purchase, securities, and insurance in the second book (On Justice) of his treatise *On Justice and Right* (*De iustitia et iure*). This volume offers a translation of the Latin text of chapters 21 (On Sale-purchase) and 28 (On Suretyship, Insurance, Pledge, and Mortgage). The edition of 1621, published by Plantin-Moretus at Antwerp, serves as the textual basis for this translation, since it was the last edition revised by the author before he died.[3] For almost half of the questions (*dubitationes*) contained in Lessius' chapter on sale-purchase we were able to rely on an unpublished

2. For an extensive overview of the literature on economics, ethics, and law, especially in the early modern Spanish empire, see J. Barrientos García, *Repertorio de moral económica, 1526–1670: la Escuela de Salamanca y su proyección* (Pamplona: Eunsa, 2011).

3. An online version of the 1621 edition can be consulted through the digital platform of the State Library of Bavaria in Munich (http://www.digitale-sammlungen.de).

modern edition and an earlier translation.[4] Yet, no full English translation of Lessius' chapters on sale, let alone of his chapter on legal securities and insurance, has appeared before.[5] The questions from the discussion on sale that have been added to the partial translation published in the *Journal of Markets & Morality* are mainly juridical in nature. Legal issues also predominate the newly translated chapter on securities and insurance.

There have been at least three reasons for integrating the more juridical-technical parts on sale and the discussion on securities and insurance into this translation. First, scholastic economic analysis and moral thought start from a legal framework.[6] Hence, it is not possible to fully grasp their insights in business and morality without fully acknowledging the juridical-technical aspects of their work. Second, the last decade has witnessed a boom in interest in early modern scholastic authors among legal

4. Wim Decock, "De 'homo oeconomicus' ontketend in Lessius' denken over markt en prijs? Editie, vertaling en studie van *De iustitia et iure*, lib. 2, cap. 21," 2 vols. (master's thesis, Catholic University of Leuven, 2005), 1:81–129; W. Decock, "Leonardus Lessius on Buying and Selling (1605). Translation and Introduction," *Journal of Markets & Morality* 10, no. 2 (2007): 433–516.

5. A paraphrastic summary in German of a miscellany of passages in Lessius' *De iustitia et iure* dealing with economic problems ranging from bills of exchange to tax policy was provided by Toon Van Houdt in *Leonardus Lessius'* De iustitia et iure. *Vademecum zu einem Klassiker der spätscholastischen Wirtschaftsanalyse*, ed. B. Schefold (Düsseldorf: Handelsblatt, 1999), 103–42. Also, an integral German translation of Lessius' *De iustitia et iure* is being prepared by Klaus Wille and Nils Jansen at the Institute for Legal History at the University of Münster (http://www.jura.uni-muenster.de/go/organisation/institute/rechtsgeschichte/rg1/lessius-projekt.html).

6. On the interconnection between economic, moral, and legal thought in early modern scholastic writings, see the introduction to this series by Jordan J. Ballor and Stephen J. Grabill, pp. vii–xvii in this volume.

historians and philosophers of law.[7] Therefore, legal scholars will be happy to read Lessius in English translation not only to get an idea of how business ethics was practiced at the time of the rise of capitalism, but also to discover the seminal contribution of early modern theologians to the development of legal doctrine. Third, there is a fundamental connection between principal contracts, such as the sale of real estate, and accessory contracts used to secure them, such as suretyships, insurance, and real securities including pawn and mortgage. Usually, businessmen and economists are not expected to care much about those contractual issues. However, the 2008 financial crisis has painfully reminded us of the paramount connection between principal contracts such as the sale of real estate and accessory agreements involving mortgages to secure those contracts. Legal securities, then, are essential in creating a stable economic environment.[8]

This introduction provides background material necessary to read the translated texts in their proper historical context. First, the life and times of Lessius will be sketched. Second, a brief explanation will be given of the techniques used by the early modern scholastics to solve moral questions arising in the marketplace. Third, Lessius' view of just pricing, business, and law will be discussed. The introduction concludes with a reflection on the way Lessius can be a source of inspiration for today.

---

7. For example, T. Duve, M. Lutz-Bachmann, C. Birr, A. Niederberger, *Die Schule von Salamanca: eine digitale Quellensammlung und ein Wörterbuch ihrer juristisch-politischen Sprache: zu Grundanliegen und Struktur eines Forschungsvorhabens*, The Salamanca Working Paper Series 1 (2013), http://publikationen.ub.unifrankfurt.de/frontdoor/index/index/docId/32401, including references to further literature.

8. The crisis has led to increased awareness about the legal construction of the marketplace. See K. Pistor, "A Legal Theory of Finance," *Journal of Comparative Economics* 41 (2013): 315–30, http://dx.doi.org/10.2139/ssrn.2262936.

Leonardus Lessius: Life and Works

Ever since Joseph A. Schumpeter's favorable account of Lessius in his *History of Economic Analysis*, historians of economic thought have endeavored to unearth the hidden treasures of pre-Smithean economic analysis in his treatise *On Justice and Right*—an endeavor that turned out to be quite fruitful indeed.[9] Eminent scholars such as John T. Noonan, Raymond de Roover, Barry Gordon, and Louis Baeck agree, for example, that his elaborations on "lack of money" as a just title to demand interest clearly prefigure the modern principle of "liquidity preference."[10] He has even been declared a father of the capitalistic spirit.[11] Yet while Lessius has been adorned with the epithet "master of economic analysis" in some biographical portraits of recent

9. J. A. Schumpeter, *History of Economic Analysis*, ed. Elizabeth Boody Schumpeter (1954; repr., London: Allen & Unwin, 1972), 99. This father of historians of economic thought was introduced to Lessius by his student B. W. Dempsey, who had included a substantial contribution on Lessius in his *Interest and Usury* (Washington, DC: American Council on Public Affairs, 1943), 144–229.

10. J. T. Noonan, *The Scholastic Analysis of Usury* (Cambridge, MA: Harvard University Press, 1957), 351–52; R. de Roover, *Leonardus Lessius als economist: de economische leerstellingen van de latere scholastiek in de Zuidelijke Nederlanden* (Brussels: Paleis der Academiën, 1969), 21; B. Gordon, *Economic Analysis before Adam Smith: Hesiod to Lessius* (London: Macmillan, 1975), 250; L. Baeck, *The Mediterranean Tradition in Economic Thought* (London: Routledge, 1994), 190.

11. It is on the basis of writings such as Lessius' *De iustitia et iure* that H. M. Robertson defended the case for a Catholic rather than a Protestant birthplace of the spirit of capitalism in his *Aspects of the Rise of Economic Individualism: A Criticism of Max Weber and His School* (Cambridge: Cambridge University Press, 1933). Cf. W. Decock, "The Catholic Spirit of Capitalism? Contrasting Views on Profit-Making Through Capital Investment in the Age of Reformations," in *Law and Religion: The Legal Teachings of the Protestant and Catholic Reformations*, ed. W. Decock, J. Ballor, M. Germann, and L. Waelkens (Göttingen: Vandenhoeck & Ruprecht, 2014), 22–44.

decades, in the early twentieth century attempts were made to start a canonization process and make him look a saint detached from the material world.[12] The mainstream and hybrid picture we retain, then, for the moment, is that of Lessius as an economist and a saint. But let us turn to the facts first.[13]

Born in Brecht near Antwerp in 1554 in the heyday of the commercial revolution in the Spanish-ruled Southern Netherlands that followed, among other things, the discovery of the Americas, Lenaert Leys (latinized as Leonardus Lessius) seemed destined to become a successful businessman. At least that was the project his guardian and uncle, Huibrecht Leys, originally had in mind before Lenaert received a scholarship in 1567 to study arts at the University of Leuven. Upon graduating as primus in 1572, Lenaert dazzled the hopes of his family and friends for a second time by entering into the freshly founded and still highly controversial Jesuit order, which sent him to Sint-Omaars (Saint-Omer) for two years of novitiate training. At the age of twenty he was appointed lecturer in Aristotelian philosophy at the Jesuit Collège d'Anchin in Dowaai (Douai), where he remained for eight years and acquainted himself also with ancient languages, biblical studies, classical literature, and Romano-canon law. He moved to Luik (Liège) in 1582 to begin theological studies, which, importantly, would lead him to spend one year in Rome at the Collegio Romano.

His stay in Rome from May 1583 till April 1584 would prove to be vital for the development of his thought. At the Collegio Romano he would take lessons with Franciscus Suarez (1548–

12. A cult especially promoted by C. Van Sull in his hagiographic *Léonard Lessius de la Compagnie de Jésus (1554–1623)* (Louvain: Museum Lessianum, 1930). A meritorious effort to unlock the economist in Lessius is R. Beutels, *Leonardus Lessius (1554–1623): Portret van een Zuidnederlandse laatscholastieke econoom. Een bio-bibliografisch essay* (Wommelgem: Gulden Engel, 1987).

13. For which we rely on Toon Van Houdt's contribution in *Nationaal Biografisch Woordenboek* (Brussels: Paleis der Academiën, 1992), 14:416–24.

1627) and Robertus Bellarminus (1542–1621), to name but two of the revered professors of the central Jesuit university, and meet Maffeo Barberini (1568–1644), the future Pope Urbanus VIII, among many others. He turned back to Luik, however, to prepare a course on scholastic theology that he would give at the Jesuit College of Leuven for the next fifteen years.[14] Crucially, Lessius took Thomas Aquinas' *Summa Theologiae* and the *Enchiridion sive manuale confessariorum et poenitentium* of Martinus de Azpilcueta (also known as Dr. Navarrus) as a starting point for his teaching activities, which turned out to be a competitive advantage in attracting students from the Leuven University to take lessons with him—a point of friction that added up to the already serious doctrinal tensions with the university due to Lessius' quarrel with Michael Baius (1513–1589) on grace and free will.[15] Lessius was accused of falling prey to "semi-peligianistic" tendencies in fanatically adhering to the "molinistic" doctrine on grace and free will of his colleague Ludovicus Molina (1535–1600). In contrast to the Augustine-based, rather pessimistic view of human nature formulated by Baius, who might be seen as a proto-Jansenist, Molinism implied a highly optimistic view of the role and capacities of the human will and intellect in gaining salvation.

From 1600 until his death, Lessius could almost entirely devote himself to the publication of his theological oeuvre ranging from

14. Lessius was not a professor, then, at the University of Leuven. The unfortunate title "S. Theol. in Academia Lovaniensi Professore" added to his name on the title page of his *De iustitia et iure* has erroneously led many a scholar to hold the opposite.

15. Lessius' lasting conflict on grace and free will with established theological authority is documented in E. J. Van Eijl, "La controverse louvaniste autour de la grâce et du libre arbitre à la fin du 16ième siècle," in *L'augustinisme à l'ancienne faculté de théologie de Louvain*, ed. M. Lamberigts (Leuven: Leuven University Press, 1994), 207–82, and X.-M. Le Bachelet, *Prédestination et grâce efficace: Controverses dans la Compagnie de Jésus au temps d'Aquaviva (1610–1615)* (Louvain: Museum Lessianum, 1931).

dogmatic, political, and moral theological treatises to ascetic and mystical literature. The only didactic activity he obviously still had to take charge of in view of his reputation as "The Oracle of the Netherlands" were the weekly debates on controversial ethical issues (*casus conscientiae*). Lessius claimed these disputations to be the hallmark of the Jesuit order and a crucial part in the practical training of future priests. It is worth mentioning that an anthology of moral questions settled by Lessius himself as a regular consultant of merchants and political leaders was added under the title *Auctarium complectens variorum casuum conscientiae resolutiones* to his posthumously published lectures on the first and third book of Thomas Aquinas' *Summa theologiae*, the *Praelectiones theologicae de beatitudine et actibus humanis* (1645). The theoretical, foremost juridical principles that should underlie the solution of any case of conscience are described in his monumental and well-known treatise on the cardinal virtues: *De iustitia et iure ceterisque virtutibus cardinalibus*, which in principle is a commentary on the *Secunda secundae* of Thomas' *Summa theologiae*. Though dwelling on the virtues of prudence, fortitude, and temperance too, the better part of the treatise includes a systematic treatment of the virtue of justice and, particularly, of property, torts, and contract law. Hence, the treatise is commonly known under its abbreviated title: *De iustitia et iure*. First published in 1605 by Ioannes Masius, numerous reprints and slightly altered editions followed at the Plantin-Moretus press in Antwerp and at other printing houses all over Europe until the nineteenth century.[16]

Lessius' obstinate defense of Molinism is reflected in the persistency with which he clung to his views regardless of the difficulties he met, even within his own order. Although he had finished it by 1602, his treatise *De gratia efficaci, decretis divinis,*

16. For an overview of the different editions, see T. Van Houdt, *Leonardus Lessius over lening, intrest en woeker. De iustitia et iure, lib. 2, cap. 20. Editie, vertaling en commentaar* (Brussels: Koninklijke Academie, 1998), xviii–xxv.

libertate arbitrii et praescientia Dei condicionata could only be edited in 1610 after internal censors had staunchly refused to accept it in its original form. Even the final, published version stirred controversy and was rejected by his friend and colleague Robertus Bellarminus, who had still defended him some years before in his controversy with the Leuven faculty of theology. Nevertheless, Lessius stuck to his point and repeated his optimistic belief in human nature ten years later in the mystical work *De perfectionibus moribusque divinis*—once again followed by fierce condemnation. Lessius, then, was used to controversy. In many other, apologetic works, he had been forced to combat the Protestant heresy and atheist ideologies with utmost doggedness in defense of the pope and the one true Catholic faith.[17] But it might well be that, in the end, some fatigue led him to dedicate his mind to genres more readily accepted by the Roman censors. Among the flood of spiritual literature that flowed from his pen,[18] one stands out: the *Hygiasticon*. Published in 1613, and followed by several translations in modern languages throughout the centuries, this book contains health tips and diets that will enable a person to grow old without losing his or her mind

17. See *Quae fides et religio sit capessanda consultatio* (1609); *De Antichristo et eius praecursoribus disputatio*, with the second disputation examining the new theological doctrines defended by Martin Luther, Ulrich Zwingli, Menno Simons, and John Calvin (1611); *Defensio potestatis Summi Pontificis* (1611); *Discussio decreti Magni Concilii Lateranensis* (1613); *De providentia Numinis et animi immortalitate* (1613).

18. *Disputatio de statu vitae deligendo et religionis ingressu* (1613); *De bono statu eorum qui vovent et colunt castitatem in saeculo* (1615); *De summo bono et aeterna beatitudine hominis* (1616); *De perfectionibus moribusque divinis* (1620). A summary of Lessius' mysticism posthumously appeared under the title *Quinquaginta nomina Dei seu divinarum perfectionum compendiaria expositio* (1640). Lessius made a translation of Dionysius Areopagiticus, too, and wrote an account of the Dutch mystical movement around Johannes Ruusbroeck, the *Apologia pro scriptoribus mysticae theologiae*, both of which works are lost to us.

and by conserving full vitality. It did not prevent Lessius from suffering from a chronic disease, which led to his death in 1623.

Foundations of Moral Problem Solving in Early Modern Scholasticism[19]

Lessius' prolific and colorful record as an author urges us to reconsider the traditional, monochromatic picture of him either as a proto-economist isolated from any theological background or a saint too pious to engage in worldly affairs. Of late, an attempt has been made to overcome this artifical dichotomy by depicting Lessius simply as the model mediator between heaven and earth he had become through fully internalizing the spirituality of St. Ignatius of Loyola, which he had solemnly vowed to follow as a young man.[20] In their pursuit to find God in all things, to bring his message to all corners and cultures of the world, and to bridge the gap between the active and the contemplative life, the Jesuits developed a sharp eye for real-world experiences and for the need of guiding the laity in their quest for a devout Christian life in their daily, down-to-earth occupations.[21] Legal analysis played a fundamental role in this endeavor.[22] It is not a coincidence that in 1600 the first autonomous treatise of moral theology, *Institutiones Morales*, was written by Ioannes Azorius S.J., nor that the moral-juridical genre of treatises *De iustitia et iure* was brought to perfection in the hands of the famous Jesuit

---

19. This section is based on a more detailed study in Decock, "De 'homo oeconomicus' ontketend," 54–78.

20. See the biographical account in T. Van Houdt and W. Decock, *Leonardus Lessius: traditie en vernieuwing* (Antwerp: Maria-Elisabeth Belpaire, 2005), 11–54.

21. J. W. O'Malley's *The First Jesuits* (Cambridge, MA: Harvard University Press, 1993) itself reads as an illustration of this thesis.

22. W. Decock, "From Law to Paradise: Confessional Catholicism and Legal Scholarship," *Rechtsgeschichte—Legal History* 18 (2011): 12–34, http://dx.doi.org/10.12946/rg18/012-034.

trio Ludovicus Molina, Leonardus Lessius, and Ioannes de Lugo (1583–1660). In their universities and colleges across Europe, the future economic, political, and scientific elite was educated, and many a merchant or prince allowed himself a private Jesuit counselor and confessor. Lessius, in particular, served as an adviser of Albert and Isabel, the Habsburg archdukes governing the Southern Netherlands during the last twenty years of his lifetime.

In drawing up a theoretical framework for dealing with the qualms of conscience their "clients" faced, the Jesuits adopted much of the wisdom developed earlier on in the sixteenth century by Dominican friars such as Franciscus de Vitoria and Dominicus de Soto at the University of Salamanca, and professors such as Ioannes de Medina in Alcalà de Henares.[23] In all parts of Europe, Thomas' *Summa Theologiae* was taken as the reference work par excellence to deal with moral problems effectively, though the Aquinate primarily served as a useful tool, given its systematic and juridical bias, more than as an authority studied for its own sake.[24] Accordingly, the revived Thomism both in Iberian scho-

23. We deliberately do not reduce the Iberian influences to a so-called School of Salamanca. Though it is beyond doubt that the University of Salamanca, which can pride itself in scholars such as Franciscus de Vitoria and Dominicus de Soto, has played a vital role in the innovation of Iberian scholasticism, the Thomistic drive that underlies it had already been started at other intellectual centers in Spain, and we should not forget the contributions of other universities such as Coïmbra and Alcala de Henares. A monumental study dedicated to the School of Salamanca and clarifying some of the myths surrounding it is J. Belda Plans, *La escuela de Salamanca y la renovación de la teología en el siglo XVI* (Madrid: Biblioteca de Autores Cristianos, 2000).

24. A decisive moment in the Thomistic revival was Pieter Crockaert's (ca. 1450–1514) decision to replace Petrus Lombardus' (1095–1160) *Libri sententiarum* with Thomas' *Summa theologiae* as a handbook for theological studies at the University of Paris in 1509. Soon afterward, a flood of commentaries on Thomas' *Summa* were spawned, of which Cardinal Cajetan's (1469–1536) stands out as one of the most influential.

lasticism and early modern Jesuit ethics was distinctly "hybrid," blended as it was with Romano-canon, humanist, and nominalist influences. The importance of Roman and canon law for the Catholic moral theologians in the early modern period can scarcely be overestimated, since it provided them with the necessary juridical categories and technical vocabulary to come to grips with moral reality.[25] As such, all commercial behavior was grasped under property and contract law, with specific transactions being reduced to their corresponding contractual forms.[26] In this manner, the early modern scholastics were obliged to deal extensively with contract law.[27] The humanist influence in Jesuit thought, both on their beliefs about humanity and on their use of an elegant Latin language, is obvious from the eminent place the classics occupied in their educational program. Consequently, it would make no sense to indict the Jesuit scholastics for linguistic barbarism or unworldliness, connotations all too frequently evoked by the term *scholastic*.[28] As for the nominalist influence,

25. See R. Savelli, "Modèles juridiques et culture marchande entre 16e et 17e siècles," in *Cultures et formations négociantes dans l'Europe moderne*, ed. F. Angiolini and D. Roche (Paris: EHESS, 1995), and B. Clavero, *La grâce du don. Anthropologie catholique de l'économie moderne* (Paris: Albin Michel, 1996), 93–108. This might give us a clue, too, as to why Lombardus' *Sententiae*, void of juridical tools, was replaced by Thomas' *Summa theologiae*, which is pervaded by Romano-canon law; thus B. Löber, "Das spanische Gesellschaftsrecht im 16. Jahrhundert" (PhD diss., University of Freiburg, 1965), 8–9.

26. The eminent legal historian James Gordley goes even so far as to detect the roots of modern property, contracts, and tort law in the treatises *On Justice and Right* of scholars such as Soto, Molina, and Lessius. See his compelling *Foundations of Private Law: Property, Tort, Contract, Unjust Enrichment* (Oxford: Oxford University Press, 2006), and *The Philosophical Origins of Modern Contract Doctrine* (Oxford: Clarendon Press, 1991).

27. W. Decock, *Theologians and Contract Law: The Moral Transformation of the* ius commune *(ca. 1500–1650)* (Leiden: Nijhoff, 2013).

28. As to the humanist-Ciceronian flavor of the language used by the late scholastic authors in general, see J. IJsewijn and D. Sacré, *Companion to Neo-*

it brings us to the heart of early modern problem solving in the Jesuit order: casuistry and probabilism.[29]

So how is Lessius going to decide the lawfulness or immorality of a particular business practice? First of all, he is going to see to the natural-law precept that in commercial relationships commutative justice (*iustitia commutativa*) should prevail, implying that in any exchange equality (*aequalitas*) between what is given and received is to be preserved. Commutative justice aims at establishing an equivalent relationship between the goods exchanged in the business transaction, without taking into account any personal conditions of the parties to the contract.[30] In buying and selling, maintaining equality will amount to demanding the just or equal price (*pretium iustum seu aequale*), established either legally by a decree of the authorities or in the market itself by the common estimation of prudent businessmen. In any case, the just price needs to reflect a series of market factors, such as the abundance and scarcity of the good in question, the number of buyers and sellers, the particular mode or type of selling, and the overall money supply.[31] Yet while this scheme surely provides us with a robust standard by which to judge particular business

Latin Studies, pt. 2, *Literary, Linguistic, Philological, and Editorial Questions*, 2nd ed. (Leuven: Leuven University Press, 1998), 289–90. J. Mahoney rightly points to the Jesuit spirit of Renaissance and humanist optimism as the main ground for their Pelagianistic and probabilistic ethics; see Mahoney, *The Making of Moral Theology* (Oxford: Clarendon, 1987), 299.

29. A selection of specialized literature, on which the account of casuistry and probabilism in the next paragraphs is based, includes A. Jonsen and S. Toulmin, *The Abuse of Casuistry: A History of Moral Reasoning* (Berkeley: University of California Press, 1988); E. Leites, ed., *Conscience and Casuistry in Early Modern Europe* (1988; repr., Cambridge: Cambridge University Press, 2002); and M. W. F. Stone and T. Van Houdt, "Probabilism and Its Methods: Leonardus Lessius and His Contribution to the Development of Jesuit Casuistry," *Ephemerides Theologicae Lovanienses* 75 (1999): 359–94.

30. Lessius, *De iustitia et iure*, 2.1.2.9.

31. Lessius, *De iustitia et iure*, 2.21.1 and 3.

transactions, it might turn out to be too general and vague. Take the following case: A buyer requests me to sell my good on the spot, whereas in fact I intended to sell it not until ten months later, being pretty sure that by that time its price would have doubled.[32] Am I obliged to sell at the current market price, or would it be permissible for me to demand a surplus, given that I am giving up a realistic profit in the future? Alternatively, is it licit for me to deviate from the current just price by virtue of the particular circumstances constituting my specific case?

It is licit indeed, according to Lessius and other sixteenth- and seventeenth-century moral theologians, to deviate from the just price in circumstances like these. To understand why, we need to consider the casuistical trait of early modern problem solving. Under influence of the nominalist tendency to value singular and concrete experiences, the early modern scholastics made a distinction between solving a moral dilemma from a merely theoretical point of view on the one hand and deciding it in practice on the other. So although on a dogmatic level any dictate of natural law is absolutely not to be broken, by considering the empirical field of application of the law, right reason (*recta ratio*) might come to the conclusion that the transaction under scrutiny actually belongs to a specific class of paradigmatic cases that through their singularity are removed from the field of application of the natural-law precept.[33] To come back to the merchant who gives up a future profit by selling in advance, his situation can be classified as an instance of the paradigmatic case in which a businessman rightly deviates from the just price by virtue of the extrinsic title cessant gain (*lucrum cessans*). The gradual but steady expansion of these so-called extrinsic titles

32. Cf. Lessius, *De iustitia et iure*, 2.21.4.28.

33. The natural-law precept itself, then, is not being abolished according to Lessius. Cf. T. Van Houdt, "Tradition and Renewal in Late Scholastic Economic Thought: The Case of Leonardus Lessius (1554–1623)," *Journal of Medieval and Early Modern Studies* 28, no. 1 (1998): 64–65.

enabled the scholastics to account for new developments in business practice and to escape the merciless rigidity of a general normative framework. Strictly speaking, any deviation from the equality principle vis-à-vis the just price in buying and selling would be illicit, but by virtue of typical circumstances, extrinsic to the contract itself, this deviation may become entirely licit, not to say imperative.

Thus nominalism introduced a significant empirical element into Jesuit moral reasoning, enabling them to bridge the gap between theory and practice. Challenging the traditional idea that human reason is capable of discerning a certain and indisputable moral order, nominalism also forced the early modern scholastics above all to approach natural law within a context of fundamental doubt and uncertainty.[34] From its practical analysis of natural law, fallible right reason cannot derive either absolute certainties or indisputable moral precepts. Human beings can merely formulate frail opinions about the existence and extent of a natural-law imperative, and persuade themselves of the respective probability of these opinions. In addition, nominalism very much took the view that morality is a matter of conflict, more specifically between an individual human being born in liberty to do as he pleases, and his powerful Creator, who is always able to restrict the liberty of human beings by a dictate of his sovereign will. Consequently, any moral agent is constantly haunted by doubts and fears, both on a speculative and practical level, about the existence of a natural law infringing upon his freedom. Recognizing that it is impossible to settle all moral questions once and for all in theory, moral theologians such as Lessius set out to dam the flood of scruples by providing confessants at least with a minimal degree of practical certainty. To

34. F. Gómez Camacho, "El pensamiento económico de la escolástica española," in *El pensamiento económico en la escuela de Salamanca*, ed. F. Gómez Camacho and R. Robledo (Salamanca: Universidad de Salamanca, 1998), 227.

this end, Lessius made a careful distinction between probable and improbable opinions concerning the lawfulness of certain actions, making it clear that any deed deemed probable could be followed in practice, even though on a speculative level its lawfulness remained doubtful.[35]

Now it is crucial, of course, to do three things: to grasp the exact meaning of *probable*, to know how this expert culture of theologian-advisers functioned, and, last but not least, to qualify some of our statements in light of the historic development of the probabilistic method.[36] What happens when the opinion of an expert about a moral act is deemed probable (*probabilis*)? Contrary to what its misleading translation in modern languages might suggest, *probabilitas* is not directly connected to mathematical-statistical certainty. In point of fact, the concept of probability indicates that a certain opinion is supported either by authority or by good rational argument. Therefore, an opinion is probable if it is endorsed by one or more authoritative scholars, or if it is the likely conclusion of sound and tight reasoning. The appeal to authority often loses out to logical argumentation in Lessius' dialectic solution of cases of conscience. Yet in any event, plurality of opinions, rational authority, and expert knowledge are central to the probabilistic moral problem-solving method.[37] Let us try to imagine what happened when an agent doubting the righteousness of an act went to consult a moral theologian such

35. Lessius, *De beatitudine, de actibus humanis, de incarnatione Verbi, de sacramentis et censuris praelectiones theologicae posthumae. Accesserunt eiusdem variorum casuum conscientiae resolutiones* (Lovanii, 1645), 19.6.7.45.

36. The most solid and extended account of the history of probabilism is R. Schüssler, *Moral im Zweifel*, vol. 2, *Die Herausforderung des Probabilismus* (Paderborn: Mentis, 2006).

37. R. Schüssler, "Scholastic Probability as Rational Assertability: The Rise of Theories of Reasonable Disagreement," *Archiv für Geschichte der Philosophie* 96 (2014): 202–31; D. Schwartz, "Probabilism Reconsidered: Deference to Experts, Types of Uncertainty, and Medecines," *Journal of the History of Ideas* 75 (2014): 373–93.

as Lessius. This professional problem-solver, much like a lawyer before the external court, informed his client about the different probable and improbable opinions with respect to his question and about the chances of violating moral precepts. At the end, within the boundaries of the set of probable opinions, the client could choose to follow the probable authority or good argument he thought was most plausible—the moral agent enjoyed plenty of freedom, then, with the expert adviser merely guiding him through the tricky moral universe and forcing him to respect some minimal standards.

Now although this picture could have been taken in the office of a Jesuit consultant such as Lessius, it certainly does not suit the practice of advisers such as Soto. For the view that it is licit to follow any opinion deemed probable (*probabilis*), that is, even if other opinions credited with a higher degree of probability exist, holds only true for *probabilism* in the narrow sense of the word. The rupture in moral problem solving brought about through its first formulation in 1577 by the Dominican Bartholomaeus Medina (1528–1580) radically separates the more liberal business ethics embraced by a younger generation of predominantly Jesuit scholars from the rather cautious advice given by earlier sixteenth-century theologians. The earlier theologians stuck to a "probabilioristic" position in solving moral problems, implying that in case of doubt, man has the obligation always to follow the more probable opinion (*probabilior*). The probabilists, on the contrary, maintained that a moral exigency to follow the most probable opinion did not exist. Medina argued that to follow a probable opinion is simply good enough and adequately safe, since an opinion is called probable when it can be followed without reprehension or vituperation.[38] Also, if people were obliged to follow the safest path, any merchant would be forced to forgo

38. Decock, *Theologians and Contract Law*, 75.

business altogether, and instead imitate the life of Christ, since that is undoubtedly the safest way of behaving, as Lessius said.[39]

This is not to say, of course, that our Jesuit would not have dreamed of a world in which people strive at more lofty ideals. Yet however paradoxical it may sound, he entertained the strong conviction that this goal would rather be attained by imposing only minimal moral standards on individuals, than by burdening the conscience of man with endless and highly specified precepts.[40] For the former approach would create the free mental space necessary for any human being to do acts of supererogation out of his own liberal choice, whereas the latter attitude would end up being counter-productive by aggravating feelings of scrupulosity and by stifling all spontaneous creativity to do good deeds. As such, in his practice as a moral consultant, the theoretical foundations of which are laid down in his treatise *De iustitia et iure*, Lessius contented himself with describing the minimal rules of conduct (*praecepta*) a merchant had to observe.[41] Yet in preaching from the pulpit and writing his spiritual oeuvre, he definitely kept alive the dream of Christian businessmen obeying more noble counsels (*consilia*).[42]

Lessius' Concepts of Usury, Just Pricing, and the Market

To sum up, then, we might submit that the interdependence of Christian economic thought and the idea of human freedom—cleverly identified by Alejandro A. Chafuen as a general characteristic of Iberian scholasticism—was even deepened by

39. Lessius, *De beatitudine*, 19.6.7.44.

40. Lessius, *De beatitudine*, 19.6.7.44.

41. Decock, *Theologians and Contract Law*, 73–82.

42. On the "double" morality of the Jesuits, see T. Van Houdt, "De economische ethiek van de Zuid-Nederlandse jezuïet Leonardus Lessius (1554–1623): een geval van jezuïtisme?" *De zeventiende eeuw* 14, no. 1 (1998): 27–37.

the probabilistic attitude of the Jesuits at the turn of the seventeenth century.[43] What is more, because of his sharp eye for existing economic reality, and in view of his commitment to stimulate prudent merchants in their wealth-creating business, Lessius refined the very legal device to come to grips with the singularity of real-life cases of conscience: the theory of the extrinsic titles or legal grounds, deriving from specific circumstances exterior to the contract itself, which allow a deviation from the equality principle in economic exchange. As has been demonstrated by Toon Van Houdt, in broadening the field of application of extrinsic titles already recognized in the scholastic tradition (e.g., "cessant gain") and, at the same time, formulating a new one ("lack of money"), Lessius almost entirely approved of the general market practice of claiming non-excessive interest in lending money.[44] Thus, Michael Novak's statement that although they felt bound to treat interest-taking more warily than did later capitalist thinkers, Iberian scholastics still discerned many legitimate forms of interest, holds all the more true in the case of Lessius.[45] Given that the usury problem pervaded the entire economic thought of the scholastics, as other contracts were constantly suspected of being artificial devices to conceal

43. See A. A. Chafuen, *Christians for Freedom: Late-Scholastic Economics* (San Francisco: Ignatius, 1986), recently republished in a slightly modified version as *Faith and Liberty: The Economic Thought of the Late Scholastics* (Lanham, MD: Lexington, 2003). See also F. Gómez Camacho's *Economía y filosofía moral: la formación del pensamiento económico europeo en la Escolástica española* (Madrid: Síntesis, 1998). These works constitute the main general introductions to late-scholastic economic thought.

44. Van Houdt, *Leonardus Lessius over lening, intrest en woeker*. Our sketch of Lessius' usury doctrine in the next paragraph is largely based on Van Houdt's analysis, pp. 231–50 (English summary on pp. 251–55). For an excellent introduction in English, see T. Van Houdt, "Money, Time and Labour: Leonardus Lessius and the Ethics of Lending and Interest Taking," *Ethical Perspectives* 2, no. 1 (1995): 11–27.

45. Michael Novak, foreword to Chafuen, *Christians for Freedom*, 10.

a money loan, it will be useful now to analyze its phantom form in Lessius' *De iustitia et iure*.

As with any other contract, a loan must be concluded according to the principles of commutative justice, requiring that equality in exchange should be preserved. Since time was not thought to have a value-creating function of its own, this implied that in due time the borrower was obliged to return exactly the same quantity of money that he had received. Any surplus stemming immediately from the loan contract (*ex vi mutui*) was considered to be a usurious profit. The casuistical turn of the late scholastics, however, urged them to modify this general scheme. They acknowledged that there could be extrinsic reasons to make it licit for the moneylender to indemnify himself by charging interest on top of the principal, namely, damage incurred, cessant gain, and capital risk. Damage incurred (*damnum emergens*) concerned the damage the lender suffered from parting with his money during the term of the loan. For if his house collapsed, for instance, he would be forced to borrow money himself at a cost.[46] In addition, money offers the possibility of making profits through investments. As a merchant abandons these lucrative opportunities in lending out his money, he is entitled to indemnification under the title cessant gain (*lucrum cessans*), which represents a sort of modern opportunity cost.[47] Thirdly, since the debtor might become insolvent by the time of repayment, the lender is allowed to demand compensation for the uncertainty he exposes himself to.[48] By the time Lessius edited his treatise *De iustitia et iure*, damage incurred and cessant gain were widely accepted titles by the moral theologians. Yet it is only with him that risk of capital was gaining solid ground.

In what was an important move, Lessius took the view that cessant gain could be invoked without further qualification

46. Lessius, *De iustitia et iure*, 2.20.10.

47. Lessius, *De iustitia et iure*, 2.20.11 and 12.

48. Lessius, *De iustitia et iure*, 2.20.13.

by any moneylender. Traditionally, an appeal made to cessant gain to demand interest had to be substantiated and stipulated separately before the loan contract was concluded. A merchant, then, needed to demonstrate that the money he was asked to lend out had actually been destined for another purpose. On top of this, the factual opportunity cost underlying the appeal to the extrinsic title had to be judged in retrospect by a wise man. However, referring to common business practice at the Antwerp exchange, Lessius made possible a general and unconditional appeal to cessant gain, even for professional lenders and bankers. On the other hand, it should be noted that in a sale-purchase contract he would still require the parties to explicitly mention the extrinsic title by virtue of which they want to deviate from the just price. For otherwise the other party could be mistaken about the real value of the merchandise, or even prefer not to enter into the contract altogether.[49] In any event, as concerns the traditional doctrine on interest and usury, Lessius undermined it even further by introducing a new extrinsic title: lack of money (*carentia pecuniae*).[50] Since determining the right amount of interest by virtue of an individually determined opportunity cost had lost its sense through the generalization of cessant gain, the value of parting with one's money had to be established on a more general level too, that is, in the abstract money market. As such, interest became the market price of money, ensuing from the economic fact—later theorized by Eugen von Böhm-Bawerk (1851–1914)—that present money is worth more than absent money. Accordingly, money has a time-value fixed through common estimation in the market. Money becomes a commodity like any other good to be bought and sold at a just price in a depersonalized market.

49. Lessius, *De iustitia et iure*, 2.21.4.27.

50. Lessius, *De iustitia et iure*, 2.20.14, especially the argument as developed in num. 123–25.

In short, it is clear that Lessius' introduction, however careful it might have been, of the new title lack of money undermined the traditional usury doctrine. This innovative title carries with it the revolutionary potential of subsuming the theory of interest under the doctrine of just pricing, and of rebaptizing usury as any interest exceeding the just price of money—which brings us to the second cornerstone of late scholastic economic thought. Lessius' doctrine of just pricing and the market stands out through the utmost consistency with which it is applied both to cases to be interpreted as sale-purchase contracts, and to cases involving other contracts, which then are reduced to a sale-purchase contract. In the latter way, our Jesuit expanded the scope of the just-price doctrine so as to further block the doctrine of usury. For Lessius, there is no doubt that a bill of exchange (*cambium*) or an insurance contract (*assecuratio*) are to be ranged under the heading of sale-purchase.[51] Consequently, the phantom of usury, by definition bound up to a loan contract, should not too readily be seen to intervene in them. The same holds true for the public auctions where bills of debt or obligations (*chirographa*) are exchanged at prices lower than their intrinsic value. Lessius convincingly argues that these bills are to be considered as saleable goods fetching a normal market price, and not as concealed, usurious money loans.[52] In the case of credit sale and purchase with advance payment too, he contents himself with formulating the common opinion that these contracts are

51. Lessius, *De iustitia et iure*, 2.23 (introductory note) and 2.28.4.24, respectively.

52. Lessius, *De iustitia et iure*, 2.21.8. In a completely unconvincing way, however, he suddenly returns to the traditional (and safe) argument of concealed usury to condemn the practice. A "deconstruction" of this maneuver is offered in W. Decock, "De 'homo oeconomicus' ontketend," 291–302, and idem, "L'usure face au marché: Lessius (1554–1623) et l'escompte des lettres obligataires," in *Le droit, les affaires et l'argent: Célébration du bicentenaire du code de commerce*, ed. A. Girollet (Dijon: Société pour l'histoire du droit, 2008), 221–38.

to be interpreted as concealed money loans, but in the end tries to show how these modes of sale-purchase are finally ruled by rational price mechanisms of their own that escape the dreary logic of concealed usury.[53] Last but not least, he analyzes the baratas-mohatras contract, a complex and artificial construction of sale and repurchase clearly devised to evade the interest prohibition, to constitute a real sale-purchase.[54]

Now how did Lessius conceive of the just price and the market? It is important to stress from the outset that *just* means "equal" or "equivalent" here (*pretium iustum seu aequale*).[55] A just price guarantees a balanced or equivalent relationship between the two constitutive elements of a sale-purchase contract, that is, between merchandise (*res*) and price (*pretium*). It is a moral-juridical concept, then, rather than the buttress of a mathematical model of economic reality gravitating towards a long-term equilibrium market price. Even so, the just price is not entirely void of the economic science. The normative account given of what a just price should be clearly reveals an analytical insight into the functioning of what nowadays we would call the competitive market price. For, by definition, a just price—even if fixed by a decree of the public authorities[56]—should reflect a number of market circumstances, such as the abundance and scarcity of goods, their objective and subjective utility, the number of buyers and sellers, the costs a businessman incurs in obtaining, transporting, and storing his merchandise, the money supply, and the mode of selling. We have the strong impression that the latter factor, representing the insight that there are different types of markets functioning according to their own logic, is

53. Lessius, *De iustitia et iure*, 2.21.6 and 7.

54. Lessius, *De iustitia et iure*, 2.21.16.

55. Cf. Lessius, *De iustitia et iure*, 2.21.2 (title).

56. If the public authorities are notably ignorant in adapting the legal price to changed market circumstances, the merchants have a right to disobey it; cf. Lessius, *De iustitia et iure*, 2.21.2.14.

increasingly occupying a central role in Lessius' moral evaluation of business practice.[57] By recognizing, for instance, that an auction is a singular mode of selling governed by its own particular mechanisms, Lessius would approve of gross fluctuations in prices established in such a market, although in view of traditional doctrine it would have been doubtful to denote a price swinging so elastically as being just.[58] By the same token, Lessius indicated that it is extremely difficult to condemn sale-credits at prices exceeding the normal just price. For there are certain mechanisms attached to the sale-purchase of particular goods, such as a bulk of cacao imported from the American colonies, which naturally lead to the creation of a distinctive mode of selling inducing a higher price. In view of the public good, colonial wares like these are imported in massive quantities, but logically cannot be sold to the wholesalers except on credit, since they first have to retail them in order to get money. And as a matter of market logic, allowing the first buyers to pay on credit attracts them in large numbers and boosts the market price.[59] In sum, it is very typical of Lessius' analytical genius first to discern the underlying economic mechanisms of a particular business practice and, subsequently, to integrate this insight into his normative judgment.[60]

---

57. In this respect, one could argue with Langholm that Lessius fulfilled a process of depersonalization or objectivization, starting with Cardinal Cajetan, who thought it more important to look at the *modus vendendi* than to the *causa contractus* for a moral evaluation of business practices. See O. I. Langholm, *The Legacy of Scholasticism in Economic Thought: Antecedents of Choice and Power* (Cambridge: Cambridge University Press, 1998), 99. I have further developed this idea in "Lessius and the Breakdown of the Scholastic Paradigm," *Journal of the History of Economic Thought* 31 (2009): 57–78.

58. Lessius, *De iustitia et iure*, 2.21.4.35.

59. Lessius, *De iustitia et iure*, 2.21.6.56–57.

60. It should not come as a surprise, then, that the normative value of commercial praxis (*consuetudo seu usus mercatorum*) occupies pride of place

Still we need to take into account Chafuen's reminder that one must exercise great care in jumping to the conclusion that in late scholasticism the just price always equaled the market price in conditions of perfect competition.[61] In the end, Lessius stressed too that the estimation of the said market factors should be carried out by intelligent, experienced, and prudent businessmen. There remains a personal element, then, in Lessius' conception of the market, which does not allow us to think of it unreservedly as an impersonal, self-regulated mechanism.[62] From his cautious approval of different kinds of monopoly exercised within the limits of the just price emerges another feature of his economic thought that would certainly look anomalous in a modern theory of competitive equilibrium.[63] Likewise, it would be a gross simplification to reduce his account of the price mechanism to either a cost of production theory of value or a theory of subjective utility. The production theory of value would hardly square with Lessius' vision of entrepreneurship: A merchant is certainly entitled to a just reward for his work, but if he has incurred exceptionally high costs, not covered by the market price, this is not a valid excuse for him to raise his prices. It is simply a case of bad luck or imprudent behavior. Conversely, if he has encountered exceptionally low costs, he is not obliged to reduce prices. For it pertains to his good luck or to his commercial prowess.[64] On the other hand, contrary to a theory of subjective utility, Lessius maintained that it is not

in his ethics; see my "Leonardus Lessius (1554–1623) y el valor normativo de 'usus et consuetudo mercatorum' para la resolución de algunos casos de conciencia en torno de la compra de papeles de comercio," in *Entre hecho y derecho: Tener, poseer, usar en perspectiva histórica*, ed. M. Madero and E. Conte (Buenos Aires: Manantial, 2010), 75–94.

61. Chafuen, *Faith and Liberty*, 83.

62. Lessius, *De iustitia et iure*, 2.21.2.7; 2.21.2.9; 2.21.3.16.

63. Lessius, *De iustitia et iure*, 2.21.21.145 and 151.

64. Lessius, *De iustitia et iure*, 2.21.4.29.

licit to let the price merely be determined by the subjective need or desire a buyer experiences for a certain good. A just price is certainly not any arbitrary price the seller can bargain to get for his good, even in the case of exotic merchandise or luxury goods.[65] Time and again, the scholastic maxim christened by Odd Inge Langholm as the "double rule of just pricing" turns up in *De iustitia et iure*: a seller may well be allowed to account for the affective and financial damage he suffers from parting with his goods, but he is not to calculate the price of the buyer's affections, needs, and desires.[66] This definitely does not mean that the late scholastics had in mind a kind of metaphysically or ontologically determined theory of value. Following Augustine, they unequivocally recognized that the natural and economic order are to be distinguished from one another.[67]

A pearl among the cases in Lessius' *De iustitia et iure* summing up his ideas on the morality of the market is "The merchant of Rhodes" in *dubitatio* 5.[68] The case concerns asymmetrically distributed information among market participants and the question corresponding to it of whether a seller is obliged to inform the other party about his knowledge of future changes in the market circumstances. Suppose, for example, that a grain merchant arriving in Rhodes, where acute shortage of grain has led to towering prices, has come to know of other suppliers sailing to the island. Should he tell the buyers about the future abundance of goods so that they can bargain a cheaper price?

65. Lessius, *De iustitia et iure*, 2.21.3.16. Hence, Lessius does not follow the traditional late scholastic division, going back to Vitoria, between necessary and luxury goods.

66. O. I. Langholm, *Economics in the Medieval Schools: Wealth, Exchange, Value, Money, and Usury according to the Paris Theological Tradition, 1200–1350* (Leiden: Brill, 1992), 232–34. An excellent illustration of this rule is Lessius, *De iustitia et iure*, 2.21.4.26 and 31.

67. Augustine, *De civitate Dei*, 11.16.

68. An elaborate discussion of this case is included in Decock, "Lessius and the Breakdown of the Scholastic Paradigm."

Making reference to the just-price doctrine, which states that a price should either be determined by the prince or by common estimation of relevant market factors, Lessius concludes that the seller has no duty at all to reveal his private knowledge. For morality in buying and selling amounts to demanding the just price, and the just price is determined by common, not by private estimation. So even though the common estimation is based on error and ignorance, the just price ensuing from it still prevails.

Lessius' solution and further elaboration of this case about speculation and insider trading reveals at least two distinctive features of his economic thought: (1) a consistent application of the general just-price doctrine to all kinds of cases, and (2) a conception of business as governed by rules of its own that should be recognized by an ethicist who prides himself on stimulating virtuous and free-market behavior.

Commerce (*negotiatio*), or the art of making money by buying goods and selling them unchanged, is a salutary art contributing to the prosperity of the community and reinforcing the cohesion of people across the globe—thus the general view in late-scholastic economics.[69] It should be licit, then, for a merchant to reap the fruits of this labor. He should do this by playing the game of the market, that is, by playing on the fundamental licitness of exploiting the latitude of the just price. For as Lessius clarified, a just price may swing in different places and at different times between the highest (*summum seu rigorosum*), middle (*medium*) and lowest (*infimum seu pium*) just price.[70] Making just profits amounts to buying a good, for example, at the lowest just price at place or time A and selling it at the highest just price at place or time B. Now Lessius fully recognized that making profits in this way largely depends on painfully mounting a web of intelligencers who can keep you informed about market developments around the world. Not allowing a businessman

69. Lessius, *De iustitia et iure*, 2.21.1.4.

70. Lessius, *De iustitia et iure*, 2.21.2.11.

who has obtained information about the future market situation to capitalize on that is tantamount to punishing prudent and industrious commercial behavior. From his insight into the market, Lessius could not possibly expect a merchant, then, to reveal his information—an insight commonly recognized in our age, but certainly not as widespread in earlier times. Cicero and Ioannes Medina, for instance, would have made the prudent businessman look a fool by requiring him to tell about his private knowledge. Acknowledging the need to stimulate prudent businessmen drawing on their experience, intelligence, and insight into the laws of the market to anticipate opportunities, Lessius could not give way to the argument that the other party had a right to nullify the contract by reason of involuntary consent due to ignorance. What is more, Lessius would explicitly state that everyone can deceive themselves through imprudent behavior: the professional buyer should blame the ignorance on himself, because he has not been virtuous enough to inform himself about the market in which he is taking part.[71] Regularly repeating that, among professionals, the marketplace is not a realm of charity and donation, but of commutative justice and inner economic logic, Lessius was not prepared to take on a paternalistic attitude in his moral judgments.[72]

Epilogue: What We Can Learn from Lessius Today[73]

In the early decades of the twentieth century, Leonardus Lessius was revived at the Catholic University of Leuven by enthusiastic

71. Lessius, *De iustitia et iure*, 2.17.5.27, 33–34.

72. For example, Lessius, *De iustitia et iure*, 2.21.4.37 and 2.21.11.84.

73. It goes without saying that much of the argument developed in this epilogue also applies to other late-scholastic authors. Robert A. Sirico has pointed out the lasting and praiseworthy reliance of modern Catholic economic thought on late scholasticism: "Both place enterprise, human initiative, the price system, exchange, private property, the division of labor, and the liberty of contract at the center of economic life" ("The Late-

members of the neo-Thomist movement who considered him to be a source of eternal truths of natural law, which through slight adaptation to the altered social and economic reality could still serve as a clue for solving contemporary problems.[74] It will be obvious from the biographical and moral-theological contextualization of Lessius' economic thought above that such an attempt was bound to fail: the market as well as the technical tools implemented to solving moral problems in the market have changed so much that the present in some way raises a barrier beyond which history cannot project its creativity anymore. Nevertheless, we are convinced that with due respect for its peculiarities, Lessius' business ethics can still be a source of inspiration for today. We should, however, not concentrate so much on the answers, but rather direct our attention to the questions themselves that Lessius raises and the fundamental principles he honors in tackling them.

First of all, Lessius gives us an excellent example of the way in which religious beliefs and involvement in the real world can be made to enter into a dialogue. He is not, as has happened so often in history and is repeating itself in parts of the globe today, taking the easy way out of this tension by creating a dichotomy between evangelical ideals and worldly practices. On the contrary, by taking a distinctly positive view of the human person and his earthly occupations, Lessius empowers the faithful to engage themselves in just and prudent commercial activities.

Second, Lessius stimulates entrepreneurship by recognizing that industrious merchants should be allowed to profit from

---

Scholastic and Austrian Link to Modern Catholic Economic Thought," *Journal of Markets & Morality* 1, no. 2 [1998]: 122).

74. See, for example, E. Van Roey, "Le contractus germanicus ou les controverses sur le 5% au XVIe siècle en Allemagne," *Revue d'Histoire Ecclésiastique* 3 (1902): 901–46; V. Brants, "Les théories politiques dans les écrits de L. Lessius (1554–1623)," *Revue Néo-Scolastique de Philosophie* 19 (1912): 42–85.

their insights into the rules of the business game. As such, a merchant can licitly reap the fruits of painstakingly obtained knowledge and information to exploit price differences across the markets. Rewarding prudent behavior—a cardinal virtue implying intelligent analysis of the present, careful consideration of past experiences, and providence as to the future—is at the heart of Lessius' economic ethics.

Third, Lessius urges the professional merchant to drop his assertive commercial behavior as soon as he leaves the increasingly depersonalized market of professional businessmen. The power of the strong is limited by the personal dignity of the poor and weak who would be crushed in a world based on mere commutative justice. Charity should complement the narrow principle of justice from time to time. Lessius, then, refuses both religious and economic fundamentalism.

Last but not least, our Jesuit has two important messages for people priding themselves in being sound business ethicists. The liberty of the human person forbids any totalitarian attempt to prescribe in abstract and pedantic details what a person should be allowed to do or not to do. Ethicists should limit themselves to pointing out the minimal standards of conduct so that the individual is able to set free his or her own creative potential for striving at more lofty ideals. On top of this, Lessius gives us a vital example in showing that any sound judgment about the morality of the market presupposes an analytical moment in which the mechanisms of the market themselves are scrutinized. It is small wonder, then, that Lessius' *De iustitia et iure* is met with increased interest in the contemporary world of academic and professional business ethics. The translation at hand may be a further tool in exploring its riches.

On

Sale, Securities, and Insurance

Book 2, Chapter 21

On Buying and Selling[*]

[*] Thomas Aquinas, *Summa Theologiae*, II, II, quaest. 77.

Question 1

Definition of *Purchase*, *Sale*, and *Business*. On the Prohibition for the Clergy to Do Business

1. Sale-Purchase

1.1. Definition

1. A *purchase* can be defined as "an agreement under which a price is given in exchange for a commodity," whereas a *sale* is "an agreement under which a commodity is given in exchange for a price."[1] Three elements are required as to the form or substance of this contract: a commodity, a price, and mutual consensus.

1.2. Substantial Elements

A *commodity* is anything that is a possible object of a sale: all goods movable and immovable, claims and titles that are usually estimated and compared in money. Likewise all present and future goods taken as a whole, since the latter can be sold through one act, even if they cannot be donated.[2] For the free faculty to make a will is not hampered by such a sale contract, since it is

1. Dig. 18.1.1.
2. Dig. 45.1.61.

possible to make a will about a price, yet it is hampered indeed by a gratuitous donation. In the same way, a vacant inheritance is a commodity and a possible object of a sale. An inheritance, however, which has not yet been declared vacant, is not saleable, for example, when the testator is still alive. Such a sale is invalid, since it is at variance with moral decency.[3]

A *price* consists of money, which was invented to be the measure and price of all things that come under human contracts, as Aristotle teaches.[4] Money can neither be a commodity in itself, nor can it be sold as a commodity, except on the basis of its material or a circumstance extrinsic to its nature. Thus, money can be sold because it is old or beautiful, or convenient to transfer, or absent, or difficult to be claimed back, etc. Before money was introduced, sale-purchase as such did not exist, but merely barter.[5] Money was invented, however, because barter was inconvenient.

It is an agreement, since this is the more general class to which sale and purchase belong as specific types of agreement. That is to say, sale and purchase are part of a single and uniform agreement, which in itself is a specific type of agreement understood in its most general conception. For out of sale and purchase a uniform agreement emerges that essentially includes the consensus of both. However distinct those parts may be, they are so inextricably bound up with each other that it would be impossible to understand one part without understanding the other, as happens with all things so closely correlated to each other.

1.3. A Consensual Agreement

The sale-purchase contract consists of a naked agreement or arrangement between the parties involved. Delivery of the commodity or the price is not required as to its substance, since

3. Dig. 18.4.7.
4. *Ethica Nicomachea*, lib. 5, cap. 5.
5. Dig. 18.1.1.

the contract is concluded by the sole consensus of the parties.[6] Therefore, it is possible for absent people to contract, or to contract by means of a messenger, or by correspondence.[7] However, for the ownership to be transferred, a delivery is required.[8] Consequently, unless delivery on both sides has followed, the contract is still held to be invalid. For although the contract is concluded as to its substance, it still lacks the final complement at which the parties intend to arrive. Hence, whenever a punishment is imposed in buying and selling, this is always to be understood as concerning the acts concluded by either of the parties' delivery, unless the legislator holds an expressly different intention. Similarly, a stipulation is not required, since we are dealing with a contract of good faith, and neither is a written document, unless the parties wish to draw up one before or after making the contract for the sake of greater security. In the latter case, the parties are held to suspend their ultimate consensus until the arrangement is sealed in writing and reread.[9]

1.4. A Reciprocal Contract

The phrases "a price in exchange for a commodity" and "a commodity in exchange for a price" clearly indicate that this contract is reciprocal, and that it requires a counter-promise or mutual consent.

1.5. Delimitation from Other Contracts

In this respect sale-purchase differs from donation and liberal promise as well as from all other contracts in which an interchange of things other than commodities and prices takes place,

---

6. See above, book 2, chapter 17, question 2, and Dig. 18.1.1 toward the end.

7. See, again, Dig. 18.1.1.

8. This is clear from what was said above in chapter 3, question 3.

9. See the teachings of Gomezius, *Commentaria variaeque resolutiones iuris civilis, communis, et regii*, tom. 2, cap. 2, num. 17.

as in exchange, loan, and all innominate contracts. Similarly, lease and hire are different, since the thing that is said to be leased or hired is not given in return for a price, but only conceded for use, even though it might seem as if the use itself is sold in a certain sense, because it is conceded in return for a price. Properly speaking, however, it is not said to be sold, since it is the thing that can be used rather than the use itself that is the subject of the contract.

2. What if both money and a good are given in exchange for a good (e.g., 100 guilders and a house in exchange for another house?) Will that qualify as a sale? Answer: It will qualify as an exchange if the good that is given is worth much more than the money. However, if the money is worth much more, it will qualify as a sale. For the qualification is based on the bigger part. If both are of equal or nearly equal value, then the qualification of the contract will depend on the intention of the parties.[10]

1.6. Sales Tax

3. It follows that when a tax is imposed on a contract of sale, it is due instantly once the parties have reached an agreement, even if the good has not been transferred yet or the price has not been paid. For the tax is owed on a fully concluded contract, and this contract is concluded as soon as the mutual consent is verbally expressed. This is the case when the consent is absolute and the price has been determined.

1.7. Conditional Consent

When the consent is conditional, the contract is suspended until the condition is fulfilled. Once the condition is fulfilled, the contract is concluded, in such a way that by virtue of a legal fiction its result (i.e., an absolute obligation) is deemed to have taken effect retroactively from the date of the beginning of the

10. Gomezius, *Commentaria variaeque resolutiones*, num. 10

contract. It would be as though the consensus had been absolute from the start.[11]

This is all the case when the condition is fortuitous. Things are different, however, with a potestative condition, since there is no retroactivity.[12] A condition is called fortuitous if its fulfillment is not in any way within the power of the debtor, but is dependent on the occurrence of a fortuitous event (e.g., ships coming from India this year). It is potestative when its fulfillment lies solely within the power of the debtor (e.g., accepting guardianship or resigning from office in my favor). The reason behind this is that it is the intention of the party imposing the potestative condition to urge the other party to quickly fulfill it. That is why there does not have to be any retroactivity once the condition is fulfilled. The contract will only start from that point on, as though it was only entered into at that moment. Otherwise he would not be stimulated to fulfill the condition more quickly. For it would make no difference if he fulfilled it rapidly or slowly, because the obligation would retroactively start from the beginning of the contract anyway. This reasoning no longer holds when a fortuitous condition is imposed on a contract. This is because the party imposing this condition would immediately want to enforce the absolute obligation, if the condition were to present itself. He returns to the occurrence of the conditional event, so that when the condition is fulfilled, he wants everything to proceed as if the condition had existed all along.

Contracts are to be interpreted according to the specific type of condition, unless it is clear that the contracting parties had other intentions. They can agree that fortuitous conditions have no retroactive effects or that potestative conditions do. But in those cases, it has to be expressed explicitly, for when it is in doubt it has to be presumed otherwise, as I have said before. Hence,

11. Dig. 20.4.9; Dig. 20.4.11; and other legal texts.

12. Bartolus' commentary on Dig. 20.4.9*pr* and, extensively, on Dig. 41.3.15*pr* and the following.

it happens that also the tax is owed retroactively, and must be paid to the person acting as the tax collector at the moment of the conclusion of the contract, not at the moment of fulfillment of the condition.

1.8. Ratification by a Third Party

As with conditional agreements, when a contract needs ratification by a third party, the contract will not be considered concluded until it is ratified, even if it appears to have been initiated absolutely. For the law provides that such a contract contains a tacit condition, which has to give power to that contract and conclude it. When that condition is met, the contract is concluded, but in such a way that this conclusion and the obligation it entails are deemed by virtue of a legal fiction to work retroactively, as though all had been so from the start, because everything has to be executed in the same manner.[13]

1.9. Determination of the Price

The contract of sale is not completed if the price is not determined (e.g., when contracting parties leave it to the assessment of a third party). Nevertheless, the contract is valid before the price is determined, so that no party can back out of the agreement without mutual consent. However, the contract is still not completed.[14] This is the reason why no taxes are owed before the price has been determined. Yet, there is no retroactivity here, because the contract was absolute and was not subject to conditions or ratification. Due to the lack of a determined price it was merely incomplete.[15]

---

13. *Liber Sextus* 5.13.10 and Cod. 4.28.7 where it is elegantly explained, and from many other laws cited by Gomezius, *Commentaria variaeque resolutiones iuris civilis, communis, et regii*, tom. 2, cap. 11, num. 30, where he discusses this theme at length.

14. Inst. 3.23, § *Pretium*.

15. For more on this, see Gomezius (cited above) and Molina, *De iustitia et iure*, tom. 2, disput. 337.

2. Business

4. "Business [*negotiatio*] is the activity through which a man acquires goods with the intention of making profits by selling them in a completely unaltered state." This is the definition maintained by Chrysostom and the canonists.[16] They conceive of selling in a very wide sense, so as to include even barter, given that for the barbarians business consisted in barter, and that money changers are doing business by bartering money.

Business is not illicit as such, but rather indifferent, since it can be directed toward a good, bad, or indifferent goal, as Divine Thomas Aquinas demonstrates.[17] Against Thomas, you might object along with Chrysostom that "by evicting the sellers and buyers from the temple, the Lord has made it clear that a merchant can never please God and hence that no Christian should be a merchant." However, Divine Thomas replies that what Chrysostom has in mind is a man for whom profit constitutes the highest goal, a man who is prepared to commit mortal sin to make a profit (what most businessmen do) or, put differently, a man who is doing business by having recourse to fraud and perjury.

3. The Prohibition for Clerics to Do Business

Clerics are not allowed to engage in business, which Gelasius makes clear when he says that "clerics should abstain from unworthy profit and should steer clear of all inclinations for any business whatsoever or they should be immediately forced to abstain from their clerical office, regardless of their rank."[18] The same is made clear in other canon law provisions, some of which draw on St. Jerome or St. Augustine.[19] In one of them, the pope says that "he

16. Chrysostom, *Hom.* 38 *in Matthaeum* 21, and *Dec. Grat.* Dist. 88, c. 11.

17. Thomas, *Summa theologiae*, 2a2ae, quaest. 77, art. 4.

18. *Dec. Grat.* Dist. 88, c. 2.

19. *Dec. Grat.* Dist. 88, c. 8 (based on Jerome); *Dec. Grat.* Dist. 88, c. 9 (based on Augustine); *Dec. Greg.* 3.1.16; *Liber Sextus* 3.24.2.

forbids monks or clerics from doing business with the intention of making profit on pain of excommunication." This clearly shows that it is mortal sin for clerics to give much attention to business. All this bears on clerics who have received holy orders. As to the monks, the prohibition goes for them in general.[20]

The church is so strict in prohibiting this because, first of all, it is so unbecoming for clerics to devote themselves to making a profit. Moreover, it completely takes over the mind and distracts them from their spiritual tasks. Also, it is fraught with risks of perjury, fraud, and injustice. That is why Ecclesiasticus 26 says that "there are two things that seem to me to be difficult and perilous: it is difficult for a merchant to keep himself from becoming negligent" (i.e., in matters that lead to salvation) "and a tradesman shall not obtain justification from sin." St. Paul says the same thing more clearly: "if we have food and clothing, we should be content with that." He supplies the reasoning in the next lines: "those who want to get rich fall into temptation, into the trap of the devil, and into many useless and harmful desires that plunge man into ruin and destruction. For lust is the root of all evil."[21]

5. Clerics can procure goods as material out of which they create something else and then sell, because this does not qualify as business.[22] This way, members of religious orders used to make baskets, mats, and the like to sell and sustain themselves with the price. St. Paul even took on the trade of making tents. Likewise, clerics can tend to their own fields to sell its fruits. They can cut out or dig up stone or metal from their land and can choose to shape it into a particular good or not. They can keep livestock on their farms in order to make money from the offspring, milk, or

---

20. Noted by Medina, *De poenitentia, restitutione et contractibus*, tom. 2, cap. *De rebus restituendis*, quaest. 30, causa 2, at the end.

21. Paul, 1 Timothy 6.

22. As Chrysostom explicitly says in the text cited above.

wool, or to sell the full-grown and fattened animals themselves.[23] For these are all in a sense fruits of their fields.

6. They are still not allowed to hire someone else's farms or similar fruit-bearing goods in order to sell its fruits and make a profit. Because although it does not qualify as business, it is strictly forbidden by canon law.[24] This is not the case if it is necessary for their sustenance. Nor are they allowed to administer or take care of a secular house.

It is not sinful for clerics or clergyman to do business through a third party that manages the entire enterprise, for instance by investing money in a company of merchants. For in that case the reason behind the prohibition no longer holds, because they are only forbidden to engage in business by themselves.[25] However, it does seem to be rather unbecoming of the ecclesiastical position, which is why I think it should not be done unless there is a just cause to excuse it.

---

23. As is rightly pointed out by Medina, *De poenitentia, restitutione et contractibus*, tom. 2, cap. *De rebus restituendis*, quaest. 30, causa 2; and by Molina, *De iustitia et iure*, tom. 2, disput. 342.

24. *Dec. Greg.* 21, q. 3, c. 1–4 (partly based on the First Council of Carthage).

25. Molina, as cited above.

Question 2

The Equal or Just Price of Saleable Goods

1. Definition

7. The *just price* is considered to be that price which is determined either by the public authorities in consideration of the common good, or by the common estimation of people. A price, then, is imposed in one of two ways.

2. Two Ways of Imposing the Just Price

2.1. By the Prince: The Legal Price

The prince or magistrate fixes the price at which a particular good is to be sold by considering all the circumstances on which the estimation of goods depends, lest the buyers be deceived or forced to give in to the sellers' whims. The doctors call this price the legal price, as though it were laid down by law. It is obvious that this price is to be considered just (except maybe for the case in which the price certainly came about through the hope of obtaining favors, discrimination against the sellers, or gross ignorance). For whatever the public authorities decide by virtue of their office cannot be called into question by the subjects, which is exactly the case with the legal price. Just as in other circumstances it is the responsibility of the public authorities to promote the common good, likewise in business they should prevent fraud and the exploitation of the poor. In addition, superiors are better informed about all the circumstances causing the estimation of the goods to rise or to fall.

8. ***Circumstances to be considered in determining the just price***—Some of these circumstances relate to the commodities themselves: their scarcity or abundance, the common need for them, and their subjective utility. Next, there are circumstances pertaining to the seller: his labor, the expenses, the risks, and the damages he incurs in obtaining, transporting, and storing the goods. Furthermore, the mode of selling plays a role, namely whether the commodities are offered spontaneously or sold on demand. A final factor concerns the buyers, whether they are few or many, and whether there is lack or abundance of money.

2.2. By the Common Estimation of People: The Common or Natural Price

9. The price is imposed by the common estimation of knowledgeable people. Hence, some call it the common price. Others speak about the natural price, as though it were constituted by natural prudence. It applies to those goods that have not received a price by the public authorities. From Digest 35.2.63 it is obvious that this price is just. There it is stated that "the prices of goods are defined neither by affection nor by private advantage, but rather in common." The reason thereof is that private judgment is fallible and easily perverted by love of gain, whereas a common judgment is less subject to error. Since this rule is the most reliable guideline available, we should observe it. The common estimation is realized by taking into account all the circumstances mentioned above in number 8.[1]

3. Differences between the Legal and the Common Price

3.1. The Legal Price is Indivisible

10. It should be noted that a clear distinction between these two kinds of prices exists in that the legal price is indivisible in its nature, whereas the common price admits of a certain latitude.[2] The reason thereof is that the legal price is fixed by one or more people who reach unanimity, whereas the common price depends on the assessment of many people who do not judge entirely in the same way. For example, what some estimate to be worth 9, others estimate 10, and still others 11.

3.2. The Common Price is Threefold

11. Hence, according to common doctrine, the common price is threefold: it consists of the lowest (also called pious), the middle, and the highest (alternatively called rigorous) price. For instance, with respect to a middle price of 10, the lowest is 9, and the highest is 11; with respect to a middle price of 100, the lowest is 95, and the highest is 105.[3] Each one of these prices again admits of a certain latitude.

---

1. Compare Martinus Azpilcueta (Doctor Navarrus), *Enchiridion sive manuale confessariorum et poenitentium*, cap. 23, num. 78 and following; Ioannes Medina, *De poenitentia, restitutione, et contractibus*, tom. 2, cap. *De rebus restituendis*, quaest. 31; Didacus Covarruvias a Leyva, *In tres variarum ex iure pontificio, regio et caesareo resolutionum libros*, lib. 2, cap. 3, princ.

2. As is taught, among others, by Ioannes Duns Scotus, *In quattuor libros Sententiarum*, lib. 4, dist. 15, quaest. 2, art. 2.

3. Covarruvias, *In tres variarum*, lib. 2, cap. 3, num. 1.

3.3. Practical Consequence

12. When the price is laid down by law, it is illicit to accept a price that exceeds the legal price. Otherwise, restitution should be made. If, on the other hand, the price depends on the common estimation, it is licit to demand either the lowest, the middle, or the highest price as the occasion permits.

4. When Common and Legal Price of the Same Good Differ

You might ask what to do if the legal and the common price do not correspond with each other. Say the legal price is 10, while the common price is 8 because of abundance or scarcity of buyers. Is it licit to sell for the legal price?

4.1. The Legal Price is the Higher One

13. If the legal price exceeds the common price, it is normally illicit to demand the legal price. The reason thereof is that normally a price is fixed in favor of the buyers to make sure that it is not exceeded. This does not mean, however, that the price cannot decrease if the circumstances change, and common estimation falls. Note, however, that I expressly said *normally*, because sometimes a price is fixed in favor of the sellers to make sure that a good is not underpriced. This is the case with the selling of perpetual annuities, life annuities, and similar rights that are usually not sold unless one is forced to do so by want of money. In this situation, the seller is allowed to demand the entire legal price. Moreover, if a buyer paid a lower price in that situation, he would not be safe in conscience. The reason is that the judgment of the magistrate is to be preferred over the judgment of the people, since the magistrate has fixed the price by virtue of public authority, taking into consideration the common good.

4.2. The Legal Price Is the Lower One

14. If the legal price is lower than the common price, then it is illicit to demand the common price, and only licit to demand the legal price. The reason for this is that the latter price is to be considered the true price of the good, determined by the magistrate to make sure that it is not exceeded. Note, however, that one can sell at the common price when the circumstances of abundance, scarcity, and similar factors have changed, while the magistrate remains notably negligent in adjusting the legal price. For in this case the law is held to be inequitable.[4] Yet it is not up to private persons to judge such things, unless the matter is morally evident (superiors should always be given the benefit of the doubt) as, for example, when it is certain that the magistrate has been bribed, or is ill informed about the circumstances of the commodities, or has fixed the price to discriminate against the sellers or the buyers.

4. Medina, *De poenitentia*, tom. 2, cap. *De rebus restituendis*, quaest. 36.

QUESTION 3

Is the Owner of a Good That Does Not Have a Legal or Common Price (e.g., Certain Gems, Special Dogs or Falcons, Exotic Birds, Ancient Paintings) Allowed to Sell It at Any Price He Wants?

1. Those Goods Can Be Sold at Any Price

15. Some doctors answer this question in an affirmative way: the owner of a good that does not have a legal or common price is allowed to sell it as dear as he wants.[1] Proof: First, these goods are not necessary for human life, so if a buyer is prepared to acquire them, he should be considered to pay freely what the seller demands. For, indeed, otherwise he would not have bought it at all, since there is not any necessity that forces him to buy. Therefore, the seller is allowed to accept the payment. Second, two legal maxims can be adduced to support this thesis: "Everyone is the moderator and arbiter of his own goods," and "A good is worth whatever it can be sold for."[2]

---

1. Dominicus Sotus, *De iustitia et iure*, lib. 6, quaest. 2, art. 3; Petrus de Navarra, *De ablatorum restitutione in foro conscientiae*, lib. 3, cap. 2, num. 11.

2. Cod. 4.35.21 and Dig. 36.1.1, respectively.

2. The Contrary Opinion Is Truer

2.1. The Price Should Not Be Set Arbitrarily by the Seller

16. The contrary opinion, namely that such goods should not be sold at the price arbitrarily determined by the will of the seller, is truer. Those goods should be priced according to the common estimation of knowledgeable men or through the estimation of the seller himself, provided that, in good faith, the latter considers all the relevant circumstances mentioned above.[3] Proof: First, the just price of this kind of good should be derived from the judgment of a knowledgeable merchant who considers the circumstances that affect the value of the good; but every good must be sold at a just price; therefore, it is illicit to sell a good for whatever it can be sold for. The major term of this syllogism is proven by the fact that the judgment of a knowledgeable man is the most certain guideline available in this context. Second, a good is not worth a certain price because it pleases the seller to sell it so dear, but rather because it is estimated so much by the judgment of prudent people, after they have considered all relevant circumstances. Therefore, he cannot sell at an arbitrary price. This opinion is to be confirmed because the judgment underlying an estimation should always be prudent. Now nobody can prudently judge a good to be worth a certain price solely because a seller wants to sell it so dear. Third, if the affirmative opinion were to be accepted, then a person could sell a good that in good faith he thinks to be worth 10, at 100 or 1000 as soon as he notices that a prince is interested in it and wants to buy it.

---

3. Navarrus, *Manuale*, cap. 23, num. 78; Cajetan, *In Summam Theologiae Divi Thomae Aquinatis commentaria*, ad IIam.IIae, quaest. 77, art. 1.

2.2. Affections Can Be Estimated

17. If the seller himself feels very strongly about the good, he is allowed to estimate his personal affections, provided this estimation comes about in good faith.[4]

3. Refutation of the Affirmative Opinion

3.1. The Buyer Does Not Want to Make a Donation

18. The buyer is not considered to be freely donating the amount that exceeds the just price. For it is not his intention to make a donation, but to buy and pay the real price of the good. Since nothing in the good itself corresponds to the increase in the price, it follows that the surplus must not be retained as though it were really part of the price. It is of no significance that the buyer is not urged to buy by force or necessity. For if that were the crux of the matter, it would be allowed to demand usury from a person who is not forced to lend money by necessity, but rather asks for a loan in order be able to spend money on games or similar entertainment.

You might raise the following objection: If the buyer does not intend to donate the surplus, why is it that in fact he does, though he knows that the good is not worth so much, and although he is not forced by anyone to buy? I reply that the buyer is so fond of the good that he prefers making a loss by paying the surplus rather than having to miss out on the good. Similarly, a borrower promises to pay usury in order to get that liquidity that he needs for playing games.

3.2. The Right Interpretation of the Legal Maxims

19. The legal maxims quoted have been improperly understood. The first maxim does not apply to the estimation of goods. It simply means that, as opposed to an agent, a real owner can

4. Navarrus, *Manuale*, cap. 23, num. 83.

dispose of his goods according to his own choice, even to the detriment of himself. The second maxim, namely that "a good is worth whatever it can be sold for," needs to be understood within the latitude of a just estimation, given that the justice of a price is not indivisible by its nature.

Question 4

Is It Licit in Some Cases to Sell a Good Dearer or Buy It Cheaper than It Is Worth?*

1. Preliminary Remarks: Deception Above or Below Half of the Just Price

1.1. Remedy in the External Court

20. In the external court no legal action is given to the offended if he has not been deceived for more than half of the just price. If, for instance, you sell a field currently worth 100 pounds at 70, 60, or only 50 pounds, you are unable to institute legal proceedings in order to get rescission of the sale or a supplementation of the price, since you have not been deceived for more than half of the just price. The situation is completely different, however, should you have sold your field for 48 pounds, 49, or less. Similarly, if you buy a field currently worth 100 pounds at 152 or more, you are able indeed to go to court and ask either for a restitution of the surplus you have paid or for a rescission of the purchase

* See Divine Thomas, *Summa Theologiae*, 2a2ae, quaest. 77, art. 1.

contract. Again, should you have bought the land at 140 or even 150 pounds, no legal action is available.[1]

1.2. Duty of Restitution in Conscience

1.2.1. Also for Deception Below Half of the Just Price

21. A buyer or seller who commits fraud for less than half of the just price is not therefore released from the duty to make restitution of the amount above or below the just price as a matter of conscience.[2] The reason thereof is that the surplus is not considered to be donated liberally, but only given inasmuch as it is due because of a sale or purchase title. That is, the surplus is considered to be spent as though it were part of the just price, namely as a sum equivalent and due to the value offered. Consequently, if it is not due, because it exceeds equality, it cannot be retained unless it is made up for in a convenient way through a supplementation of the price or the mending of the good.[3]

1.2.2. Rejection of Gerson's Opinion

22. From this it is clear that Jean Gerson is wrong when he takes the view that someone who deceives his contracting partner for less than half of the just price is not obliged to make restitution, though he did commit a sin and is obliged to go to confession. For he argues that an injury is not done to one who knows and wills it. Yet I disagree with this viewpoint, because

1. This is clear from Cod. 4.44.2; Cod. 4.44.8; *Dec. Greg.* 3.17.3 (Alexander III); *Dec. Greg.* 3.17.6 (Innocent III). See also Gomezius, *Commentaria variaeque resolutiones iuris civilis, communis, et regii*, tom. 2, cap. 2, num. 22, and Covarruvias, *Variarum resolutionum*, lib 2, cap. 3, num. 2.

2. Divine Thomas, at the place cited above; Divine Antoninus, *Summa Theologica*, part. 2, tit. 1, cap. 16, § 3; Ioannes Medina, *De poenitentia, restitutione et contractibus*, tom. 2, cap. *De rebus restituendis*, quaest. 32; Covarruvias and the authors quoted by him in *Variarum resolutionum*, lib. 2, cap. 4, num. 11.

3. Navarrus, *Relectio in cap. Novit de Iudiciis*, not. 6, num. 54 and following.

the offended party does not consent to the injury absolutely voluntarily, but rather in the way I explained above, namely like a borrower paying usuriously high interest. Furthermore, Gerson's reasoning is self-defeating. For if such fraud is a sin, it certainly is a sin against justice, and accordingly restitution is obligatory. Last but not least, positive law does not approve of these malpractices as though they were licit. Positive law merely tolerates them by making neither restitution nor rescission of the contract obligatory lest greater evil emerges.[4]

1.2.3. The Right Interpretation of Digest 4.4.16

23. The latter viewpoint, namely that positive law does not approve of these malpractices, is not contradicted by Digest 4.4.16, which goes as follows: "Pomponius also says that as regards the price in purchase and sale, it is naturally licit for the contracting parties to overreach each other." For this kind of overreaching is to be understood within the limits of the just price,[5] and "naturally licit" actually means that it is tolerated according to the *ius gentium*. Against this background, I will now answer the main question.

2. Answer: Legal Grounds to Deviate from the Ordinary Price

2.1. Legal Grounds to Sell Dearer

First, there exist certain legal grounds that make it licit in some cases to sell a good for a higher price than it would actually be worth and sold for in other circumstances.

2.1.1. By Virtue of Office

24. *Merchants can charge a slightly higher price*—The first legal ground is based on the specific office or job of doing business.

---

4. See the teachings of Thomas, *Summa Theologiae*, 2a2ae, quaest. 77, art. 1, ad 1, and of Bartolus in his commentary on Cod. 4.44.2 and 8.

5. Covarruvias, *Variarum resolutionum*, lib. 2, cap. 3, num. 2.

Accordingly, merchants are allowed to demand a slightly higher price than people who are not selling by virtue of office, but just occasionally.[6] The reason thereof is that one can place a monetary value on the fact that merchants constantly have to be solicitous and preoccupied about acquiring, storing, and supplying commodities, and by doing so are forced to omit many other opportunities of making profit. Therefore, a good is estimated more when sold by a merchant, who does so by virtue of his office, than when it is sold by a soldier or a craftsman, since the latter sellers only coincidentally obtain and sell the same good.

Note that this legal ground does not entail the permission to sell dearer than the legal or common price. For in the determination of the price, the office of doing business has already been taken into account.

25. If someone selling occasionally demands the same price as is usually demanded by the merchants, he is not wronging the buyer as long as the good is of equal quality. For he can sell at the current price, even though he incurred neither the costs nor the solicitude of the merchant. Anyway, it is not a necessary precondition for demanding a certain estimation that you actually suffered the particular inconveniences that gave rise to the estimation. It is not a sufficient counterargument to maintain that the goods are estimated less in the hands of a nonprofessional. For merchandise is estimated less in the hands of a nonprofessional not because it really is worth less in his hands (supposing that he has the intention of selling it at the right moment). Rather, goods get a lower price in their hands because that kind of people do not have the intention nor the knowledge to wait for an opportunity. Consequently, they throw their goods on the market themselves without having been asked by a buyer to do so.

---

6. Ioannes Medina, *De poenitentia, restitutione, et contractibus*, tom. 2, cap. *De rebus restituendis*, quaest. 31, § *Et procedit*; and Cajetan, ad IIam. IIae, quaest. 77, art.1.

2.1.2. Potential Profits Forgone, Damages Incurred, and Affections

26. Further legal grounds to sell a good dearer than it is worth of itself are potential profits forgone, and damages incurred as a consequence of the alienation of the good. By the same token, a seller is allowed to take into account his affections toward the good and the pleasure he takes in it, all of which he is deprived of through selling. The surplus should be determined according to the estimation of the profits forgone, the damages incurred, or the pleasure and the affections lost, respectively. If present, these circumstances are licit grounds to charge a surplus since a seller not only transfers the naked good itself, but also the convenience, pleasure, and affections he experiences on account of it. Consequently, a person may demand their estimation, even though the good has a legal price.[7]

27. ***Explicit mentioning of the legal title***—Note, first, that the seller should signal to the buyer the legal cause on the basis of which he demands the higher price, lest the buyer believe the good itself is worth more. For the buyer might not wish to pay for the inconvenience affecting the seller.

Reasonable affections—Note, second, that if a good is estimated more on account of the title called affections, these affections have to rest on a just reason that makes it prudent to estimate the good so much, as is the case, for example, with a very unique gem or an ancient statue. Yet, what should you do if your affections do not rest on reason, and yet you do estimate the good to be as valuable as the price you demand for it on the basis of your affections? For example, you estimate a house worth 1000 guilders at 2000 because it is a family heirloom. I answer that some permit it, given that anybody is allowed to estimate the inconveniences he suffers. However, I do not absolutely approve of these practices, since affections that lack reason need to be

---

7. As is rightly taught by Petrus de Navarra, *De ablatorum restitutione in foro conscientiae*, lib. 3, cap. 2, num. 21.

corrected. Such affections should not be paid for or made up for by a towering high price.

28. ***When you had intended to keep the good***—Note, third, that the legal ground called potential profits forgone allows you to sell dearer if you had intended to keep the good until it would be worth more, but a buyer presents himself now. In that case there are two ways of reaching an agreement.

First, you can reach an agreement about a fixed price. If it is certain that the good will be worth, say, 30 guilders at the time you initially intended to sell it, then you are allowed to sell at that price after having subtracted the estimated value of storage and risk of corruption or loss. Consequently, if you estimate the cost of storage and the risk to be only 2 guilders, you are allowed to sell at 28, or if cost and risk amount only to 1, at 29. If it is doubtful whether this good will be worth 30 guilders but certain that it will be worth between 24 and 30, then the seller is allowed to demand a price that lies between the lowest and the highest: the more certain he is, the higher the sum he can charge. This is the background against which *Decretales Gregorii IX* 5.19.6 needs to be understood: this text deals with someone who initially intended to keep his good until the future moment agreed on for payment, and states that this person is now allowed to sell the good at a price more or less than it is deemed to be worth at that future moment, that is, at the medium price in between the highest and lowest just price at that future moment.[8]

Second, you can reach an agreement about an undetermined price. In that case the seller asks the buyer to pay him what his merchandise will turn out to be worth commonly at the time he initially decided to sell his good, after having subtracted the estimation of storage and risks. However, he is not allowed to demand the highest future price, since he is not certain that he will obtain that price if he keeps his good until later. Put differently, you cannot rightly speak of profit forgone in this case.

8. Covarruvias, *Variarum resolutionum*, lib. 2, cap. 3, num. 6.

Therefore the estimation of that certainty (i.e., the price of being certain) should be subtracted from the highest price.

2.1.3. Labor and Expenses

29. ***If the good has not been estimated yet***—A third legal ground for selling dearer consists of the labor and expenses you have incurred in obtaining, transporting, and storing the goods. This is to be understood, however, for goods that did not yet have their price determined. The first time a good is priced, the seller can take into account extraordinary expenses. As in the case, for instance, of merchandise that needs to be protected against robbers by a military escort because it is transported through dangerous areas. However, I do not understand this to apply to expenses incurred through bad luck or imprudent behavior.

The condition of merchants—Another matter altogether is the case in which the goods have already received a price for which they are sold in different places, since one is obliged either to sell at the current price or to retain his goods.[9] Moreover, in the determination of the price, the merchant's labor and his ordinary costs have already been taken into account. So if a merchant has incurred more labor and expenses than are covered by the current price, that is his bad luck, and the common price cannot be increased on that account, just as it need not be decreased even if he has not incurred any expenses at all. For it belongs to the normal condition of merchants that they can make profits if they have small expenses, just as they can suffer losses if they have large and extraordinary expenses.

2.1.4. Abundance of Buyers and Money

30. Because of an abundance of buyers and money but a shortage of goods, prices are higher than under opposite circumstances, namely, when there is a shortage of buyers and

9. See Medina, *De poenitentia, restitutione et contractibus*, tom. 2, cap. *De rebus restituendis*, quaest. 31; Covarruvias, *Variarum resolutionum*, lib. 2, cap. 3, num. 3; and other doctors.

money but an abundance of goods. The reason thereof is that these factors make the common estimation of goods rise. For a thing will be dear when it is asked for by many buyers and can barely be obtained or can be obtained only in small amounts. Conversely, a thing will be cheap if it is abundantly available and few people ask for it. This is the reason why it may suddenly happen that prices skyrocket when plenty of rich and avid buyers arrive on the market, whereas prices may collapse just as quickly when these people all move away, as, for example, when all of a sudden a prince accompanied by his court visits a city, or the Indian fleet moors, as is correctly explained by Luis de Molina.[10]

Is it licit to sell dearer to foreigners?—Moreover, in the latter cases Molina does not hold to be condemned the practice whereby foreigners have to pay higher prices than the local people, if only the goods are sufficiently available. The goods are considered to be dearer for those foreigners who have plenty of money and are willing to buy a lot than they are for the local people. However, if goods are not sufficiently available, then the price indiscriminately increases for everybody. In that case, sellers that sell dearer to the strangers in order to be able to demand a lower price from the locals should not be tolerated. Actually, one could say that in both cases the price rises for everybody. No seller is obliged to sell cheaper to the locals than to the strangers. Nevertheless, it has become accepted through custom that the locals are given preferential treatment, given that the increase is sudden and transient. For it is not illicit to sell dearer to strangers than to locals, if only the limits of the rigorous price are not exceeded in contracting with the foreigners.

2.1.5. Sale in Favor of the Buyer

31. You are allowed to raise the price of a good, if you sell it only to do the buyer a favor, and if otherwise you would not have sold your good. The reason thereof is that one can place a monetary value on the fact that you sell a good that was not for

10. Molina, *De iustitia et iure*, tom. 2, disput. 346, num. 2.

sale. However, I would limit this ground to those cases in which you suffer a real inconvenience or detriment.

It should be noted that one is not allowed to sell a good dearer on account of the subjective utility or necessity that drives someone to buy your good (as is the depraved practice of many utterly immoral merchants).[11] The reason thereof is that no one is allowed to sell to another precisely that which belongs to that other person. Now the subjective utility the good offers belongs to the buyer, not to the seller. It comes forth from a circumstance of which the seller is not the cause.

2.2. Legal Grounds to Buy Cheaper

2.2.1. The Good Is of Little Use to the Buyer

32. The first legal ground to buy cheaper is that the good is of little use to the buyer and is bought in order to do the seller a favor.[12] For prices fall both because there are no buyers on the market and because the good is hardly convenient to them.

2.2.2. The Mode of Selling

33. Prices may fall based on the mode of selling—at a public auction, for instance, or when buyers are solicited to buy. For as the maxim goes, according to Cajetan, "merchandise coming onto the market without being solicited becomes a third cheaper."[13] The reason thereof is that this mode of selling betrays an abundance of goods and a lack of buyers who are willing to buy in the ordinary way, both of which factors make the price of the good fall. War booty, for example, sells cheap, just as a good that is of no use or is inconvenient to the seller.

---

11. See Divine Thomas and the common opinion of the doctors.

12. Medina, *De poenitentia, restitutione et contractibus*, tom. 2, cap. *De rebus restituendis*, quaest. 32; Navarrus, *Manuale*, cap. 23, num. 84; and other doctors.

13. Cajetan, ad IIam.IIae, quaest. 77, art. 1; Medina, *De poenitentia*, tom. 2, cap. *De rebus restituendis*, quaest. 31, § *Similiter*; Covarruvias, *Variarum resolutionum*, lib. 2, cap. 3, num. 5; Navarrus, *Manuale*, cap. 23, num. 78; etc.

34. *Annuities*—If a good has a legal price fixed in favor of the sellers (as in the case of newly created annuities), the price should not be lowered based on the mode of selling or on abundance. After all, if the same legal regime persists, a change in some of the market circumstances will not immediately bring about a change in that price. Otherwise it would be licit to buy a newly constituted annuity worth one guilder for 12 guilders, if the buyer were solicited. Now this is false, since it is at variance with prevailing law. The situation is different, however, with respect to old annuities, since for a variety of reasons their legal price has been abolished through custom, especially in Belgium.

35. *Auctions*—It may happen at auctions that sometimes the common price is exceeded because the buyers are bidding against each other. It is probable that under these circumstances a seller is not obliged to make restitution.[14] The reason thereof is that the price of goods offered for sale at an auction is fortuitous and uncertain. Subsequently, though they are mostly sold cheaply because people have no appetite to buy them or buyers are not abundantly present, sometimes it may happen that prices rise due to the presence of a multitude of buyers with a big buying appetite. It ultimately depends on good or bad luck. This opinion is to be confirmed since the just price of such a marketplace is the price that one is able to charge through that mode of selling in the absence of fraud. Moreover, it is the common practice and use of learned and pious men everywhere.

2.2.3. Abundance of Goods

36. A good can be bought cheaper if there are plenty of goods available and few buyers present, as is usually the case at the closing of the fair, particularly when there is a shortage of money in addition to this. All these factors sharply decrease the common price of saleable goods. I deliberately speak about the *common*

14. This opinion is held by the merchant community and taught by Petrus de Navarra, *De ablatorum restitutione in foro conscientiae*, lib. 3, cap. 2, num. 36–37.

price, since the *legal* price does not fluctuate so easily. For that reason, it is illicit to deviate from the legal price immediately.

2.2.4. Donation

37. A good can also be bought cheaper than the common price on the grounds of donation. For a seller may be considered to condone an insufficiently high payment, just as he is allowed to sell dearer if the buyer proposes to donate a surplus.[15] However, donation is never assumed to take place when the situation involves either ignorance of the just price or necessity to enter into the sale-purchase contract. It is strictly required that the contracting parties are informed about the prices of the good, and that they voluntarily enter into the contract in the absence of fraud and force. What is more, I believe that these requirements are not sufficient, unless the two parties are closely affiliated to each other by family bonds or ties of friendship. For donation is never to be assumed to take place between people who do not know each other, unless there are crystal clear signs of a willingness to give a gift.[16]

2.2.5. Buying a Huge Amount of Goods at Once

38. If you buy plenty of goods at once, you are allowed to buy at a cheaper price than if you had bought only a small amount of goods. The reason thereof is that you save the seller from many worries and concerns he would otherwise have had. Moreover, you make it easier for him to acquire a new stock. Selling a huge amount at once, then, is much more profitable for the seller than trading his goods one by one at the ordinary price. Consequently, this mode of buying makes the seller lower the price.

---

15. Conradus Summenhart, *Septipertitum opus de contractibus*, part. 3, quaest. 57, § *Prima conclusio* (immo *quinta conclusio*) and quaest. 58, § *Quarta conclusio* (immo *quinta conclusio*); Medina, *De poenitentia, restitutione et contractibus*, tom. 2, cap. *De rebus restituendis*, quaest. 32.

16. Cajetan, ad IIam.IIae, quaest. 77, art. 1; and Covarruvias, *Variarum resolutionum*, lib. 2, cap. 4, num. 9.

QUESTION 5

AM I ALLOWED TO SELL AT THE CURRENT PRICE EVEN THOUGH I KNOW THAT THE PRICE OF THE GOOD IS ABOUT TO FALL?

For example, if I gathered by correspondence that a great bulk of goods will be imported, or that soon a stock of goods that had hitherto been kept out of business will be brought onto the market, am I allowed to conceal this knowledge and sell at the usual price?

39. This question is debated by Antipater of Sidon and Diogenes of Babylon in the third book of Cicero's *On Duties*. Antipater says that behaving like that would go against the duty of a virtuous man, whereas Diogenes takes the other view. Both of them do not clearly express, however, whether concealing information is at variance with the principles of justice. Cicero firmly holds it is.[1] But the contrary is true. Therefore I answer as follows.

---

1. Cicero is followed in his rejection by Johannes Medina and Conradus Summenhart: see Medina, *De poenitentia, restitutione et contractibus*, tom. 2, cap. *De rebus restituendis*, quaest. 35; Conradus Summenhart, *Septipertitum opus de contractibus*, part. 3, quaest. 62, § *Tertius modus*, and quaest. 63.

1. Solution

1.1. You Are Allowed to Sell at the Current Price

40. Even though the seller knows about a future dropping of the price, and the buyer is unaware of this, the former can sell his goods at the current price without committing any injustice.[2] The reason is that a good can justly be sold at the common estimation as long as this estimation prevails. For the just price is that price which is either fixed by a law of the prince or by the common estimation. This is confirmed by the fact that the private knowledge of an individual seller alters the sense and estimation of the community just as little as the private knowledge of a buyer does. Otherwise a buyer would not be allowed to buy at the current price if he knew that prices would rise afterward. Genesis 41, however, proves this to be false, since it depicts Joseph buying up the entire grain stocks of Egypt at the current price notwithstanding his knowledge of the impending grain shortage.

1.2. Objections and Responses

Following Medina you might object, first, that in this case the common estimation is not prudent, because it has not come about through a consideration of all the circumstances determining the value of a good.

41. I respond by denying that this estimation is not prudent. It is sufficient that it came about through a consideration of the circumstances that are commonly known. And since the future cannot be foreseen by all people, it is not necessary that the estimation of a good be derived from those future events. Otherwise a good would inevitably be sold at an unfair price every time a major influx of goods is expected due to harvest,

---

2. Divine Thomas, 2a2ae, quaest. 77, art. 3, ad 4, and the commentary of Cajetan on this passage; Silvester Prierias, *Sylvestrina Summa*, part. 1, s.v. *Emptio*, quaest. 15; Dominicus Sotus, *De iustitia et iure*, lib. 6, quaest. 3, art. 2, ad 3; Covarruvias, *Relectio in Reg. Peccatum, de regulis iuris in VI*, part. 2, par. 4, num. 5–6; and other doctors.

the arrival of a fleet, or any other circumstance of which none of the contracting parties knows.

You might object, second, that goods that have been imported and are now fully present make the price fall, because an abundance of goods lowers the price. Accordingly, goods that will shortly be present lower the price too. For what is only at a small distance does not seem to be at a distance at all: it is simply considered to be present.

42. I respond that a present or imminent abundance makes the price fall indeed when people in different places know about it. This does not hold true, however, when nobody knows about the abundance. Consequently, even though there are plenty of goods at the harbor or in the city, the price does not fall as long as people ignore it. For that reason you are allowed to sell your goods at the price that still prevails.

1.3. It May Go against Charity

43. I said that he can sell his goods at the current price "without committing any injustice," because sometimes it might happen that it goes against charity, as, for example, when you sell a bulk of goods to one person who suffers serious damage from this contract so as to lose his rank and possessions. As a rule, however, it does not go against charity, since you are allowed to take care of your own interests even though as a result your neighbor will suffer a corresponding loss. (This is clearly indicated by Thomas' statement that "a seller is endowed with ample virtue if he lowers the price or communicates his knowledge about the future times of plenty."[3])

1.4. Dissimulation and Lying

Nonetheless the seller should beware of seducing people into buying by having recourse to fraud or lies. For in that case he behaves unjustly, is the cause of the buyer's loss, and as a

3. Divine Thomas, 2a2ae, quaest. 77, art. 3, ad 4.

consequence is obliged to make restitution. Such is the case when, for example, he calls in a straw man to convince the buyers that the price will soon rise. But suppose that the seller is asked if a fleet or abundance of goods is expected in the future, and he feigns not to know. I would say the seller is not obliged to make restitution, because he is not obliged to speak the truth to his own serious detriment. What is more, some believe that he would not even be obliged to make restitution if he were to say that there is not going to be any future abundance at all. For this is considered a lie by virtue of his office, told to avoid personal loss, comparable to the situation in which a beggar standing at the door of a rich man and expecting alms would tell another beggar passing by that the rich man has already performed the almsgiving. Of course, this does not apply when someone has no real interest in lying, given that the liar would be considered to have lied in order to harm his neighbor.[4] Now this opinion is probable if the seller is not to be deemed trustworthy. For a buyer who believes such a person has only himself to blame if he suffers any inconvenience as a result.

2. Cases

44. Against this background we can now move to the cases put forward by Medina. In the first case, when you know about a future siege of the city, are you allowed quickly to get rid of the goods you have stored in the city without telling the buyers about the imminent threat? In the second case, are you allowed to lease your house at the usual price even though you know that rents are going to fall because the royal court will move? And in the third case, are you allowed to sell your grain at the current price, even though you know that the magistrate has drawn up a decree to lower the price but has yet to promulgate it? The last case can be extended to the exchange and alienation of money.

4. Petrus Aragonensis, *De iustitia et iure*, quaest. 77, art. 3.

45. As regards the third case, some believe you are not allowed to sell a bigger quantity of grain than you originally intended to sell, namely, when you were still ignorant about the decree. They want the same to apply to any commodity you know will soon diminish in price because of a decree issued by the magistrate. Nevertheless, if on the basis of your knowledge you sell more than you initially intended to, they believe you are obliged to make restitution.[5] The reason is that the magistrate who revealed the contents of a decree to a single person before promulgating it publicly is obliged to make restitution if the latter took advantage of this knowledge to enrich himself to the detriment of someone else. After all, it is the magistrate who was the cause of the harm. Consequently, the seller who enriched himself as a result of it should also be obliged to make restitution, no matter how he gained the information.

46. ***The opposite opinion is truer***—Regarding the third case, the opposite opinion seems to be truer. It does not go against justice to sell more goods as a result of your knowledge of that decree.[6] Proof: Even though I know that a decree concerning merchandise or money has been drawn up by the prince or his magistrate, as long as this decree is not promulgated it does not have any obligating force. Consequently, the old price prevails. It is the same with laws in general: a newly drafted law meant to abrogate the preceding law has no force until it is promulgated. For that reason I am still allowed to sell at the old price.

47. Now you might raise another objection. I might be allowed indeed to sell in good faith at the old price until the date of promulgation, just as the other merchants, who are unaware of the decree. Yet I am not allowed to sell more goods at that price as a result of my knowledge of the decree than I would have sold otherwise. For I am not allowed to avail myself personally

5. See Molina and some jurists quoted in the former's *De iustitia et iure*, tom. 2, disput. 354, num. 7.

6. As is expressly held by Covarruvias, at the place cited above.

and at the expense of others of a law that should be common to all people.

This objection is not convincing. First, no existing law forbids me to take advantage of my knowledge of that decree. Second, whether I have been induced to sell by my knowledge of that decree or on account of another reason is of no importance as to the equality or inequality that must be preserved in making a contract. Now if I sell a bushel of grain at the current price without knowing anything about the decree, the equality between price and good will be observed. The sale will be in accordance with justice and I will not be obliged to make restitution, even though in the near future the price might be lowered pursuant to a decree. Consequently, equality will be observed and the sale will be just too, although I have come to know of the decree. Third, the inner intention cannot cause an external act that is normally just to become unjust and to require restitution.[7]

48. ***Refutation of the opinion to the contrary***—I do not accept the inference made by those who take the opposite view. It is true indeed that by virtue of his office a magistrate is obliged to try as hard as he can to prevent the kind of decrees we discussed from favoring some and harming others. From this it cannot be inferred, however, that someone who avails himself of the knowledge of these decrees is also obliged, since he is not required by virtue of his office to promote the interests of the citizens or to prevent them from suffering harm. For example, consider what happens if a magistrate excludes some sellers from the market without any reason. The price of your goods skyrockets. The magistrate is obliged to indemnify the citizens for the damage they suffered as a result of this price increase, because contrary to the duties of his office he caused the prices to rise so high. You, on the other hand, are not obliged to make compensation, because under these circumstances your goods were simply worth the price for which you sold them.

7. See above, chapter 12, number 128.

49. ***Pressure by the merchant and bribery***—However, if you are the real cause behind the injustice committed by the magistrate, that is, the exclusion of other merchants from the market, then you are responsible for the harm caused both to the excluded sellers and to the state community. The main reason thereof is that for the sake of your advantage you enticed the magistrate to inequitable practices. The same seems to apply if you bribed the magistrate so that he would inform you about the decree before its promulgation, on account of which you were able to sell your goods dearer to the serious detriment of others.

But I am not sure if the second part of this reasoning is sufficiently strong. Although the magistrate's disclosure goes against his office (and as a consequence he may be punished on that account, just as he may be punished for having violated other secrets), this does not seem to be the cause of the unjust harm, for the merchant sold his goods at the just price. Therefore, it seems that the person who disclosed the secret information is also not obliged to make restitution or compensation for the injury until he is sentenced to do so.

A similar case would be the following: In times of acute grain shortage, a magistrate is informed by mail about the arrival of supplies within a fortnight. Despite a prohibition on diffusing the information, to which all the magistrates agreed, one of them lets his friend know about the future events so that he can sell his entire stock in the meantime. The magistrate who disclosed this information does not seem to be obliged to make any compensation.

Question 6

Is the Seller Allowed to Charge a Higher Price If He Is Selling on Credit?

1. It Is Allowed within the Latitude of the Just Price

50. Within the limits of the just price it is licit to sell a good dearer on the basis of extension of payment. For example, if you would have charged the lowest or medium price in case of payment with ready money, then you are allowed to charge the highest just price when selling on credit. For all these prices lie within the latitude of the just price.

2. Legal Grounds for Charging a Higher Price

2.1. Not on the Basis of Extension of Payment Alone

51. It is illicit to demand, merely on account of the extension of payment, a price that exceeds the highest just price for which a good could have been sold in cash. This is the common opinion of the doctors. The reason thereof is that extension of payment in fact amounts to a kind of implicit loan. For extending the payment is just like lending back again the money that first you yourself have received from the debtor. Now since in a loan it is illicit to acquire anything beyond the principal, it is illicit to receive more than the just price when selling on credit.

52. ***If the future value of the good is believed to be higher***—If a good now worth 10 is believed to be worth more or less than 12 at the future moment of payment, you are allowed to sell at 12 on credit, at least if initially you had decided to keep the good until that time.[1] For in that case the seller is no longer charging a surplus on the basis of extension of payment, but rather by virtue of profits forgone. Consequently, he could even have demanded the surplus when being paid in cash—on the same assumption that initially he had intended to keep the good until later.

If the seller had no intention of selling the good in the future—In this respect, Cajetan errs when teaching that in a credit sale it is licit now to negotiate about the future, higher price foreseen at the moment of payment, even if the seller had not decided to keep his good until then. He argues that from the perspective of the buyer, the contract is accomplished as soon as he has conveyed the price. Now since the good is worth more at the time of conveyance than at the time of the agreement, the equality principle requires the buyer to pay a higher price. I respond that Cajetan's view is not in line with the common opinion of the doctors.[2] They hold that the very conveyance of the good to the buyer makes the seller lose his ownership and transfers it to the buyer. So if the price of the good rises, it rises to the advantage of the buyer. The seller is not entitled to demand his share of the price increase, unless he had intended to keep the good for himself. The common opinion does not contradict *Decretales Gregorii IX* 5.19.6 because this decree concerns a seller who had initially intended to keep his good. This is explained by the gloss and

1. As is evident from *Dec. Greg.* 5.19.6 (Alexander III), which has been discussed above (question 4).

2. Covarruvias, *Variarum resolutionum*, lib. 2, cap. 3, num. 6; and Medina, *De poenitentia, restitutione et contractibus*, tom. 2, cap. *De rebus restituendis*, quaest. 38, § *Aliam quintam*.

the common opinion of the doctors. It can also be derived from *Decretales Gregorii IX* 5.19.19, where a similar case is treated.

As to Cajetan's argument, I reply that a sale-purchase contract is essentially concluded by a verbally expressed mutual consensus. Moreover, the price of a good has to be determined according to the value of the good at the time of conveyance, namely, when the ownership is transferred to the buyer. In everyday speech, though, it is said that the contract is concluded through the payment of the price, because that constitutes the purpose and the end of the contract.[3]

2.2. On the Basis of Profits Forgone

53. It is licit to raise the price by reason of profits forgone or damages incurred through the extension of payment.[4] For as it is licit in a loan to demand a surplus beyond the principal on account of this legal ground, so it is in a sale beyond the just price, because extension of payment is a kind of implicit loan.

2.3. On the Basis of the Risk of Capital and Difficulties to Obtain Payment

54. It is also licit to demand a surplus beyond the just price on the basis of the risk of capital to which you are exposed in selling on credit. It is licit, similarly, on the basis of the expenses and troubles you fear may arise in the course of recovering the money.[5] Some doctors do not approve of the first legal ground, namely, risk of capital.[6] However, it can be defended for the following

3. See above, question 1.

4. This is clear from chapter 20, question 11.

5. Ioannes Medina, *De poenitentia, restitutione et contractibus*, tom. 2, cap. *De rebus restituendis*, quaest. 38, § *Ad tertiam causam*; Antonius Cordubensis, *Tratado de casos de consciencia* [*Summa Hispana*], quaest. 84; Petrus de Navarra, *De ablatorum restitutione in foro conscientiae*, lib. 3, cap. 2, num. 110.

6. Dominicus Sotus, *De iustitia et iure*, lib. 6, quaest. 4, art. 1; and Navarrus, *Manuale*, cap. 23, num. 83.

reasons. First, in everyone's view you can place a monetary value on the fact that you expose yourself to such great danger. Second, the seller can call in a guarantor. Now just as the latter can demand the just price of providing surety, the seller can, too, when the buyer wishes him to provide surety for payment himself.[7]

55. The following should be noted though. First, the risk must be real and not fictitious. Second, the seller is not allowed to force the buyer to make him, rather than somebody else, a guarantor. Third, the seller is not allowed to demand a price higher than the price he would be prepared himself to pay, if necessary, for passing on the risk to somebody else. Fourth, the seller should indicate to the buyer the legal title on which he bases his demand of a surplus, especially if there is doubt whether the buyer really agrees to that title. For maybe the buyer does not want to give anything on account of that specific title.

2.4. Goods Usually Sold on Credit Can Be Sold Dearer

56. There are goods that are usually sold only on credit or with payment on deferred terms. It is licit to sell them dearer than if they were retailed in cash.[8] This is the case, for example, with the commodities that are imported in massive quantities from the Indies or elsewhere and shipped off to the main ports. Subsequently they are distributed among various merchants who send them to different places where they are to be retailed one by one in cash. In Antwerp, for instance, some of the goods imported from Venice are sold on a term of 10 months, others on a term of 8; goods from Florence are sold on a term of 10

---

7. See chapter 20, question 13. There you will find a more elaborate proof and a reply to Sotus and Navarrus, who both develop the same argumentation.

8. This is derived from Sotus, *De iustitia et iure*, lib. 6, quaest. 4, art. 1, ad 4. Covarruvias, *Variarum resolutionum*, lib. 2, cap. 3, num. 6, referring to Salicetus and Decius, believes this opinion to be probable.

months; goods from Lucca on a term of 9; goods from Naples and Milan on a term of 6 or 8. In the end, of all kinds of goods, most are sold mainly on a term of 6, 8, 9, 10, or 12 months. It is not even exceptional that these terms are doubled under the binding condition that the buyer already pays half of the sum around midterm, and the rest at the end of the term.

57. The reason is that these commodities cannot be sold for ready money in quantities that are either useful to the political community or wanted by the buyers. Therefore, it was necessary to introduce a mode of selling whereby it is possible to pay on credit, that is, on deferred terms. When this mode attracts many buyers it causes the prices of goods to rise. Thus, they are not dearer only because of extension of payment. Rather, the rise in prices is a side effect of this particular mode of selling, which has the potential of attracting numerous buyers. In addition, since a price is not indivisible in its nature, it often happens that in fact the price demanded in a credit sale does not at all exceed the rigorous just price licit in a cash sale. Furthermore, extension of payment is almost always inconvenient to merchants. Not infrequently we see them negotiate in order to reduce the term agreed upon in return for a remission of about 8 or 9 percent a year, depending on the length of the term. It makes no difference that a particular merchant does not suffer this inconvenience, because that does not prevent the common price from being effective.[9]

3. Conclusion: The Just Price of Goods Sold on Credit

58. In sum, the higher prices usually charged for goods that are sold on credit cannot easily be condemned, unless they are unjust for another obvious reason. For one can rightly assume that the true price of a particular commodity in a particular mode

9. This has already been demonstrated in the preceding chapters.

of selling is precisely that price which has been imposed by the merchants in consideration of all the relevant circumstances. However, if the magistrate fixes a price, that price should be observed.

Question 7

Is the Buyer Allowed to Offer Less because of Advance Payment?

1. It Is Not Allowed on the Basis of Advance Payment Alone

59. It is illicit to pay a price lower than the lowest just price merely on the basis of advance payment.[1] The reason thereof is that this would amount to making a profit beyond the principal on account of an implicit loan. For paying in advance is like implicitly lending money now in order to be offered an implicitly usurious restitution later when the good, which will have increased in value, is delivered. The surplus value of the good as compared to the price is given by virtue of a prior agreement on the basis of advance payment, namely, on the basis of the use the seller gets of the money for the period between payment and delivery.

1. According to the common opinion of the doctors.

2. Legal Grounds to Buy Cheaper

60. It should be noted, however, that sometimes extrinsic factors make it licit to buy cheaper on the basis of advance payment. For example, if the buyer suffers loss, forgoes profits, or runs the risk of dealing with a fraudulent seller who will not respect the deadline, or delivers filthy goods, or is not going to bring them at all. A monetary value can be placed on all these circumstances. Ultimately, this mode of selling makes the price fall because it attracts plenty of sellers whereas it repels buyers.

3. The Wool Trade

61. Based on the above exposition, it is not easy to condemn the common practice of buying wool cheaper in advance. This occurs in Spain and in other regions, for an arroba of wool (which equals 25 pounds) is usually bought there in advance at a much lower price than it is worth at the time of delivery.[2] That this is licit can be proven by the following reasons.

Profits forgone—First, merchants buying on advance payment suffer a loss of profit precisely because they pay in advance. For several months before the delivery of the wool they lack the money with which they could have made profits through moneychanging activities in the meantime. A sign thereof is that they readily pay an additional one or two crowns per arroba if the seller permits them to extend the payment until the moment of delivery or even two or three months after delivery. Therefore, a buyer is allowed to enjoy a discount that equals the estimation of the profit he could have hoped to make and of which he deprived himself by paying in advance.

---

2. This practice can be defended according to Sotus, *De iustitia et iure*, lib. 6, quaest. 4, art. 1, ad 4; Cordubensis, *Summa Hispana*, quaest. 85; and Molina, *De iustitia et iure*, tom. 2, disput. 360, who very recently gave an elaborate account of the current wool practice.

Fear of perfidy—Second, merchants often fear default on the part of the seller. He might not deliver the total weight of wool promised, for instance, or he might deliver filthy or poor quality wool. A sign thereof is that buyers readily pay somewhat more than usual, say, half a crown per arroba, if they can trust the seller to bring goods of the right quality. Moreover, the more prosperous the seller will be considered to be, the higher the extra sum per arroba that the buyers are willing to pay, because that makes the buyers less fearful of default on the part of the seller. Now a monetary value can be placed on this fear. Therefore it causes the estimation of the goods to decrease.

Scarcity of buyers—Third, whereas the particular mode of selling on credit makes the price rise by attracting plenty of buyers, conversely the particular mode of selling on advance payment makes the price fall by attracting only a few buyers but plenty of sellers. For there are few who buy wool by this mode of sale-purchase, and many who sell. Therefore the price in this mode of selling is lower than if the good is delivered immediately upon payment.

The good is less convenient to the buyer—Fourth, a good that must be delivered to the buyer after a few months is worth less than a good that must be delivered to him immediately. For a present good and the immediate ownership over it offer many opportunities that a future good does not. So if he buys and gives the money at once, he is allowed to pay less than he would if he paid at the time of delivery.

62. ***Even under different assumptions, the goods would not get a higher price***—Fifth, let us suppose that sale on advance payment did not exist, for instance, because it was forbidden by a decree, or because merchants were not prepared to pay in advance. In that case the wool would not get a higher price than if advance payment had taken place. As experienced merchants claim, and as is proven by reason, the wool would rather be sold at an even lower price. For the price would fall drastically due to the huge amount of wool becoming available at the time of shearing. What is more, the sellers would try to sell the wool immediately to avoid the costs of storage and to get the money they badly need at that moment to pay their debts and buy fodder for wintertime. In conclusion, the sellers are not wronged by those advance payments since ultimately they get the same price as they would if no advance payment existed.

You might object that the value of the good at the moment of delivery exceeds the price paid in advance, and that, as a result, this price is unjust. This inference is proven as follows: The just price of a good is the value of the good at the time of delivery, and not at the time of the agreement. If I buy grain worth 10 crowns at a price of 10 through advance payment, but this grain is only to be delivered after 4 months when the grain is worth 14, then the purchase contract is inequitable and implicitly usurious, since the grain is worth more at the moment of delivery. Similarly, when buying a pound of wool at 14 crowns that in fact is worth 18 crowns at the moment of delivery, the purchase contract is inequitable and implicitly usurious. For the excess value of the good as compared to the price is a profit directly stemming from advance payment.

63. I respond by rejecting the inference made. For the just price of a good is its value at the moment of delivery, unless on external grounds the good is estimated less at the moment of contracting. This is the case, for instance, if there happen to be few buyers and many sellers because of the mode of selling at that time, or if buyers forgo profit and fear fraud and default on the part of the seller by reason of this mode of sale-purchase. In that case a good may well be considered to have a higher naked value of its own, but it still does not have a higher value because of those circumstances. In addition, the just price of a good at the moment of contracting should not be estimated according to the price at the moment of delivery. For then the price is influenced by the contracts previously concluded: due to the sale-purchase agreements on advance payment a scarcity of goods has been created till the time of delivery, and, concomitantly, prices have risen. Now since this scarcity depends on the preceding contracts, you are not allowed to take the price of the goods at the time of scarcity as a measure for the prices agreed on in the preceding contracts. Otherwise you would have to pay the price prevailing in times of scarcity even if you buy in times of abundance, but the seller is unable to deliver the good immediately, which is absurd.

64. *Consequence*—The price at the time of delivery must not be derived from the price brought about through the sales on advance payment. It must be derived from other factors, so that the good is worth that higher price at the moment of delivery even if such sales had not taken place. But that obviously is not the case. For if the wool had not been sold through many contracts of that kind, it would not be dearer at the time of delivery than it was at the time of the prior agreement. So the wool sold dear at the time of delivery is not at all the same wool as that which has been sold on advance payment. It is the wool supply which is still left and is dearer because of its scarcity. For if all the wool already sold in advance would be put for sale on the moment of delivery as if it had not yet been sold, it will not be dearer. The price of a good sold on advance payment must, however, be derived from the moment of delivery.

Question 8

May a Bill of Debt or Bond Be Bought for Less Than Its Nominal Value? (e.g., You Now Buy at 96 or 97 Guilders a Right on Payment of 100 Due Next Year)

65. I suppose that those kinds of bonds may be bought at a lower price if obtaining the payment will be difficult, risky, or very inconvenient. Profits forgone and damage incurred are equally licit titles. Yet the crux of the problem is whether these bonds can be bought at a lower price of themselves, that is, when those titles cannot be invoked. There are two different opinions on this question.

1. The Opinion That It Is Allowed

66. Some doctors contend that such bonds may be bought at a lower price.[1] It can be demonstrated as follows.

1. Panormitanus, *Commentaria in quartum et quintum Decretalium libros*, super quinto Decretalium, *De usuris* rubrica 19, cap. 6 (*In civitate*), num. 7; Innocent IV, *In quinque libros Decretalium commentaria*, super quinto Decretalium, *De usuris* rubrica 19, cap. 6 (*In civitate*); Cajetan, *Peccatorum summula*, s.v. *Usura implicite commissa*, casu 3; Navarrus, *Manuale*, cap. 17, num. 231. The same opinion was taught by the most learned Cardinal Bellarmine in Leuven and by Petrus Parra in Rome.

First, as is evident from experience, when such bonds are offered for sale as merchandise, they are estimated to be worth less than ready money by the common judgment of people. For ready money offers many opportunities that bonds do not. Consequently, they may be bought at a lower price. This inference is right because the just price of any saleable good is the price settled by the common estimation. Why not apply the common estimation to the case of the bills of debt, if in all other cases the just price is considered to be the price based on that estimation?

67. You might object that in this case the common estimation is based on the need of those who want more ready money, and that as a consequence the estimation is not prudent and inapplicable. Otherwise it would be licit to demand twice as much from a person prepared to give that sum because of his need.

Yet, the inference made in the objection is not valid. For the estimation of nearly all goods depends on the common need to which people are subjected. If this common need were absent, nearly all goods would be considered worthless, such as medicine, for instance, or food and shelter. Moreover, it is not required that this need is felt by everyone. It suffices that many or most people are in need of that good in order for the common estimation to be valid. In this particular case, those bonds are needed less than ready money and do not offer the same potential of benefits and opportunities to make a profit. Therefore, they are prudently estimated to be worth less. It does not matter that you in particular do not prefer ready money to such bonds. That is just an accidental fact. For their price does not depend on your estimation but rather on the common estimation. Likewise you could sell medicine at the common price even though you yourself are never in need of it.

68. Second, let us assume those bonds were not of lower value than ready money. Then it would follow that the sale-purchase agreements on personal annuities, which is the general practice in a great many places, are to be deemed unjust. For, indeed, these contracts amount to nothing else but buying a right to receive annually, say, one-sixteenth part of the principal so that after sixteen years the principal is restored in full. From the point of view of justice it does not matter at all whether the repayment takes place by yearly installments or by lump sum at the end of the contract. So if a right to receive 96 by 16 annual installments is worth as much as 96 in ready money, it will be illicit for the buyer of the annuity to receive anything beyond that sum after the sixteenth installment has taken place. Neither will it be licit for the buyer to receive the principal in full if the seller wants to buy back the annuity. In that case the installments already paid should be subtracted from the entire principal. However, both of these inferences run counter to the current practice in plenty of provinces where the papal bull of Pius V has not been adopted. And it is utterly harsh to condemn that practice as being inequitable.

69. Third, it is stated in Digest 50.17.204 that "it is less to have an action than to have the thing." Bonds, then, are of less value and can be bought cheaper. Because of the danger of concealed usury at this point some doctors add that this view should not be accepted as a general rule. It should only be applied with regard to annuities having a price fixed by a public law or a common estimation and to other rights that have already been issued before. For example, if Peter owes me 100 guilders payable in two years by virtue of a loan or a sale-purchase contract and I want to sell my bill of debt to you, then you are allowed to buy my right for 97 or 98 guilders.

But can the debtor himself buy the bill of debt so as to release himself of his obligation? I respond that the debtor is allowed to buy. If the creditor offers that bill of debt for sale, there seems to be no reason for banning the debtor from buying that bill in the same way as anybody else.[2] For the debtor need not be put in a condition worse than that of other people in buying the bill of debt.

2. Navarrus, at the place cited above.

70. ***Unless the debtor caused the trouble***—However, this does not apply in the case where the debtor is the immediate cause of the sale because of his unwillingness to pay. Then he is not allowed to buy at the same price that anybody else would pay. The reason thereof is that he is obliged to stop making trouble and make clear that payment will pass off smoothly and safely upon completion of the term. Consequently, he cannot estimate the debt to be lower on account of the trouble he causes. Others, however, can, because they are not causing the trouble and hence are not obliged to stop it.

2. The Contrary Opinion Is Safer

The other opinion is truer, namely, that buying such bonds cheaper is not allowed. It is the common opinion of the doctors.[3] It can be demonstrated as follows.

71. First, this opinion is more widely accepted and the common opinion of the doctors. I also hold this view.

Second, a debtor who owes 100 guilders and pays less for the bill (say, 96) commits usury because of the anticipation. For he implicitly lends 96 until the payment date, and then receives 100, since the debt of 100 guilders is extinguished. Now this is exactly what happens when someone buys a bond worth 100 guilders at the price of 96. Consequently, it follows that this is also usury. You may object that the major term of this syllogism may be true if the buyer pays less merely on account of his anticipating the payment date. The situation is different, however, if he pays less because he acts not like the payer of a debt but as the buyer of someone else's right—a right that in the whole community is neither estimated nor sold dearer whenever it is put up for sale as

3. Medina, *De poenitentia, restitutione et contractibus*, tom. 2, cap. *De rebus restituendis*, quaest. 38; Sotus, *De iustitia et iure*, lib. 6, quaest. 4, art. 1, ad 4; Silvester, *Silvestrina summa*, part. 2, s.v. *Usura* 2, quaest. 14; Gabriel Biel, *Collectorium circa quattuor libros Sententiarum*, lib. 4, part. 2, dist. 15, quaest. 11, art. 3, dub. 4.

merchandise. Of such importance is the legal title or the form on the basis of which the contract is made. I respond that this seems to be more of a distinction in the mind than in the thing itself.

72. Third, if the buying of bonds at a lower price were accepted, then all kinds of usury could be cloaked. For a usurer could maintain that he is not willing to enter into a loan of consumption but still is prepared to buy a right on 100 or 200 guilders. And every borrower is able to impose this duty on himself.

You may object that there will not be concealed usury if such a right or claim is bought by the usurer for a price not lower than the price for which it is publicly sold with collateral. I respond that I have already discussed this possibility and disapproved of it in practice.[4]

An unconvincing addition to the objection is the following: The objection should not be applied in cases where someone imposes upon himself the duty to pay a certain amount with the explicit intention to sell this duty immediately afterward as a right (except for the case of the constitution of annual rents). For this mode of contracting is not common, as the more straightforward way is to conclude a loan for consumption. Consequently, this behavior is rightly considered to be usurious. But we should make a distinction with regard to bills of debt or rights that long beforehand have been constituted for another reason. For that kind of bond is very frequently sold on the markets, and always for a cheaper price than its intrinsic value.

Yet I do not find this addition to be convincing. For in practice this distinction does not exist. If no usury is committed in the sale-purchase at a discount of an old bond, why, then, in buying a new bond? Thus the buyer of this bond is to be considered not a usurer but rather a miser and a harsh man toward his neighbor.

73. Fourth, let us assume that a right on payment of 100 guilders at the end of the year is of less value than 100 ready guilders. It will follow, then, that someone buying at 100 ready

4. See above, chapter 20, question 14.

guilders is sinning against the virtue of justice and obliged to make restitution.

Note, however, that I admit that this argument is not convincing. For its conclusion is false. First, the 100 ready guilders do not exceed the limits of the just price at all; they just fall within the rigorous price. So if someone is willing to give 100 guilders, the seller is allowed to accept that amount. Second, with this kind of bond the seller is not obliged to lower the price even though payment will be difficult. He can simply demand the intrinsic value of the bond without taking into account the difficulties or the extension of payment. For through common practice it is accepted that a seller tries to get the highest price possible as long as it remains within the limits of the amount due. The same applies to old annuities. So if he can find a buyer who has a sound knowledge of the conditions of the good and who is still prepared to give that much, then the seller can justly accept the price.

3. Refutation

The first argument in favor of the first opinion can be refuted as follows: Bonds are estimated less either because there is some risk or difficulty involved or because the buyer who pays ready money deprives himself of potential benefits and opportunities that the bond does not give him. The second argument in favor of the first opinion can be refuted in that there is always some risk involved in the selling of personal annuities by reason of the length of time. Moreover, not the yearly installments, but the right on them is bought.[5]

---

5. See below, chapter 22, question 5.

Question 9

May Bills of Debt, Also Known as *Librantiae*, Be Bought at Half the Price if Obtaining Payment Is Difficult or Uncertain?

1. Response

74. It is often right to do so, namely when obtaining payment is so difficult or uncertain that precisely on the basis of this accompanying circumstance the bills of debt are prudently estimated at half their price. For example, if a bill of debt is intrinsically worth 100, yet the attending difficulty or uncertainty is so severe that any merchant would be happy to purchase it at 50, then it can be bought for 50 or a little bit lower. Depending on the extent of the difficulty and uncertainty it may even be licit to buy it for 40 or 30.

2. If It Is Not Difficult for You in Particular to Obtain Payment

75. Even though other merchants may experience difficulties in obtaining payment, Peter and his partners will not because they enjoy the favor of the prince and his officers or have concluded contracts with him. Consequently, they should not be allowed to buy at that moderate price, since the ultimate reason for lowering the price is lacking in their case. On account of this, some believe that merchants who concluded contracts with the king are not allowed to buy bills of debt originally issued to his soldiers, or so-called *librantiae*, at a discount, at least not at a noticeable one. For they are certain of integral payment without difficulties.

76. The contrary opinion is probable and truer, namely, that this kind of bill can be bought at the lower price without committing any injustice.[1] The reason is that the market price of these bills of debt does not depend on the advantage of one person or a few people, but rather on the public estimation, that is to say, on the value they would get if they were publicly offered for sale on the marketplace with the whole town coming together and responding to the auctioneer. This reason is confirmed by the fact that these bills of debt do not have a price fixed by the law. Hence the price needs to be determined by the common estimation.

The estimation of bills of debt depends on public judgment—Therefore, if the prince of the Ottoman empire owes you 1000 guilders and there is absolutely no hope—or very little—of obtaining payment unless you invest a lot of money and effort in it, then it is licit for you to buy the bill of debt cheaply, say, at 100 or 50 guilders, even if you in particular know about a peculiar way to easily recover the integral sum. This is to be considered your good luck.

It can go against charity—Nevertheless, merchants often sin against charity if they are not willing to pay a reasonable price to poor soldiers who by severe need are forced to sell their bills of debt, whereas they themselves make enormous profits.

---

1. One of the doctors taking this view is the most learned Ludovicus Molina in his *De iustitia et iure*, tom. 2, disput. 361.

3. Remarks

77. ***Selling bills of debt for their intrinsic value***—It should be noted, however, that those who dispose of bonds can rightfully decide not to take into account the difficulty or uncertainty of obtaining payment and refuse to sell their bills of debt unless they receive the total sum. For it is prevailing custom to sell such bills at the highest possible price in the absence of fraud or ignorance and within the limits of the sum they contain.

78. ***Collectors and treasurers***—It should further be noted that these bills of debt cannot be bought at such a low price by the debtor himself or his ministers, who by virtue of their office should pay out the bonds, because they are the very cause of bad payment.[2] More often than not, the collectors or treasurers of princes commit grave sin in these matters. This is not the case, of course, if they are not the cause of bad payment and if there is no scandal.

2. See the discussion above, dubit. 8.

QUESTION 10

WHEN I SECRETLY KNOW THAT MY DEBTOR IS INSOLVENT, CAN I SELL MY BOND AT AN ORDINARY PRICE TO SOMEONE WHO IS NOT AWARE OF HIS INSOLVENCY?

1. The Opinion That It Does Not Go against Justice

79. This case occurs frequently among merchants. One could think that it is not at odds with justice, as long as buyers are not lured in with lies or deceit.

First, it is not unjust, because selling a good at its commonly estimated price is not an offense committed against the buyer (since it is considered to be the just price for the good). The sale happens in this manner, therefore it does not go against justice. Neither does it matter that the estimation is based on a mistake, for they all think that the debtor is solvent, since everyone considers him to be a wealthy man. It does not matter, because that kind of mistake does not concern the substance of the good (which would be the case if someone were to buy a fake debt-claim thinking it was real, or a glass object thinking it was a gem), but only hinges on some extrinsic quality, that is, not on some condition of the good sold, but of the person who has to deliver it. In any event, the mistake does not make the contract unjust, nor does it do away with the common price. For instance, if I sell you a good possessed by someone else, who is generally considered a good man, with the burden that you have to recover it from him, while I know that you will have to take great pains to recover it, then no one is going to say that this sale is unjust. For it is not the seller's responsibility to explain the conditions that are extrinsic to the good if he is not asked about them. It is the responsibility of the buyer to inquire about them and to take everything into consideration.

80. Second, it is not unjust, because the person selling his merchandise at the current price, knowing that a vast amount of the same merchandise will be on offer in the market in a short while, does not sin against justice, even if the value is based on a mistake or ignorance.[1] So by the same token, the person selling such a bond at a price at which it is commonly estimated among merchants will not sin against justice either, even if the estimation stems from mistake or ignorance. Accordingly, just as that merchandise is worth as much as commonly estimated, so too is this bill of debt and the obligation attached to it.

Third, if I know that the enemy will destroy my crops or burn down my house, I can still sell it at an ordinary price to someone who is not aware of these facts. Yet no one would want to buy it if they knew. Thus it is not unjust to sell the letter of the debt at the ordinary price.

Fourth, if the obligation is worthless when the debtor is not able to pay, it will also be worthless when he is not willing to pay and cannot be forced to pay because he is a powerful person (for this is all worth the same, according to people's common estimation). Consequently, it would seem that I would not be able to sell at the ordinary price to some merchant who would be able to obtain payment thanks to his industry and zeal. However, from what I said in question 9 it is obvious that this is incorrect.

1. As I said in question 5.

2. The Opposite Opinion is Truer

81. Whatever your opinion may be concerning the justice of this practice, to me it seems to be absolutely illicit, since it certainly goes against charity, especially when it risks causing great harm to someone who is vulnerable. Moreover, it also turns out to go against justice. For just as the right over the fruits of a barren field is of little value in its own right and cannot be sold at the same price as the right over a fertile field, so too does the same apply to the right over an insolvent debtor. Consequently, this defect seems to be intrinsic to the good, which means that you have to notify the buyer. If you do not notify him, he can at least rescind the contract, because it was caused by deceit.[2] Things are different in the cases proposed above, since the good is not intrinsically more damaged or of less value there, yet estimated at a lower value by accident, that is, because of some extrinsic quality. From this you can derive my answer to the arguments.

2. According to what I said in chapter 17, question 5.

Question 11

Is a Seller Obliged to Reveal a Defect in the Good He Wants to Sell?

1. Assumptions

1.1. Selling a Defective Good at the Price of a Normal Good

82. It is inequitable to sell a good with a qualitative defect (unjust weight, unjust number, unjust measure) or a quantitative defect at the same price as a good that lacks a similar defect.[1] The reason is that such a contract is not based on the equality required. This sin is committed by wine sellers who mix water with wine, and by grain sellers who intermingle grain of good quality and grain of inferior quality, as for instance the salesmen in Amos 8:6 who say, "let us sell the grain of bad quality." There are also people who, by tricks, make heavier paintpots that in the end are sold as if they had not been spoiled. Many businessmen in Antwerp and elsewhere have grossly enriched themselves by applying this method. Yet the buyers are cheated and would not have been willing to pay the price asked for that quantity of goods had they known about the fraud. Finally, anyone using a

1. Thomas, *Summa Theologiae*, 2a2ae, quaest. 77, art. 2–3.

fraudulent measure commits a sin and acts against Proverbs 11:1: "False scales are an abomination to God."

83. *When mixing does not affect the quality*—Suppose that, following the mixing, the good did not become more inferior in quality than similar goods sold by others. If the seller demands the same price as the other sellers do, he cannot be condemned as a matter of justice, since in no way does he harm the buyer on account of the fraud. For, why would he not be allowed to bring his goods in the same state as the other sellers' goods are in, and, subsequently, sell them at the same price? This frequently occurs in the sale-purchase of wine, grain, and similar goods. Wine of supreme quality is mixed, then, with wine of lower quality or with water, and genuine grain with unrefined corn. This practice is allowed on the condition that the wine or grain added is not of inferior quality than the wine or grain regularly sold by other merchants. This is Lopez's opinion, even if a price has been fixed by the community.[2] Personally, I am inclined to take the view that such a person should be punished on charge of forgery and deceit. For such admixtures are fiercely hated by the community and earn the forgers themselves a bad reputation.

1.2. Buying a Precious Good at the Price of an Inferior Good

84. By the same token, it is inequitable to buy a good that does not have any defect at the price of a defective good or to buy a precious good as if it were a cheap one, as, for example, when a gem is sold as glass. This rule applies even if the seller, due to his ignorance, does not estimate his good higher than a defective or cheap one. The reason is that the contract does not preserve equality. For the seller does not intend to make a donation of the value of the good that exceeds the price that he gets. Quite the reverse, he wants to sell the good for its entire value and get a just price in exchange for it.

---

2. Ludovicus Lopez, *Instructorium conscientiae*, part. 2, cap. 42.

85. If, however, in a particular region, a good is commonly estimated cheaper because people do not know that it is highly valued elsewhere, then one can buy it there at a low price. This is notably the case in South America where gold and other precious goods are exchanged for mirrors, bells, pocketknives, and similar items. Likewise, if in a certain city gems of extraordinary intrinsic value are estimated at a low price by the local dealers, then someone may still buy them at the low price even if he knows that actually they are of great value. For in this market they are estimated to be worth no more. Finally, you are allowed to buy a bunch of herbs sold as fodder at the common price, even if you know that the bunch contains some very special herbs. The reason thereof is that the good as a whole is not worth more with respect to the specific use for which it is normally bought.

2. Response

2.1. When Asked About a Defect, the Seller Is Obliged to Reveal

2.1.1. Duty to Reveal Most Hidden Defects and Deliver a Suitable Good

86. If the buyer asks the seller whether the merchandise is of good quality and void of any defect, or if he wants the good for a specific use, then, as a matter of justice, the seller is obliged to reveal the defects of the goods that are most hidden, or to offer the good that the buyer particularly desires. This is the common opinion of the doctors. It is proven because by virtue of his office the seller is obliged to tell about the condition of his merchandise, especially when asked about it by the buyer. Otherwise a kind of fraud that buyers could not avoid would be rife. For as a general rule, nobody knows the condition of the good better than the seller himself. So when the seller affirms that the good is void of any defect or even praises its qualities, although in fact it has a hidden defect, he does injustice to the buyer.

2.1.2. Consequences

More specifically, if in this manner he has enticed somebody into the contract who would otherwise not have bought at all, the contract is invalid on the grounds of deceit causing the contract.[3]

87. If the buyer would still have been willing to buy the good, but not at the price he now paid, because he could easily have found a good that is of better quality at that price, then the contract is not invalid, since the deceit is not causing the contract itself but merely the excessiveness in the price. In this case, however, the seller must make restitution of the gap between the price he charged and the lower price for which the buyer could have acquired the good. For the deceit concerns precisely that sum.

By the same token, the seller is obliged to make restitution if he offers a good that is useless or inappropriate for the specific use the buyer wants from it. For example, when a worn-out piece of cloth is sold as if it were new, bad spices as fresh, or contaminated grain as sound.

This applies too, when the seller opens up his box of tricks to make it more difficult to detect the defects of the good so that he can sell it as if it were intact. For although in that case he is not saying anything, he is still lying about the quality of the good through his acts, as, for example, when someone pours a drop of quicksilver into the ears of a horse to make it shake off its slowness and make a good impression on a potential buyer.

2.1.3. Extent of Liability

88. ***The seller is held responsible for the ensuing damage***—In all these and similar cases in which deceit based on words or acts is the cause of the contract, the seller is held responsible for all damage ensuing from the deceit, unless he admonishes the buyer in time. This is to be understood about all damages that in all probability could have been predicted to ensue from the deceit in question. For example, if you sold a sick sheep instead

3. As can be derived from chapter 17, question 5.

of a healthy sheep, then it is likely that the whole flock has been infected, or if you sold defective building materials, it is small wonder that subsequently the whole house has collapsed.[4]

89. *Whether the contract has to be rescinded*—Is the seller obliged to rescind the contract and make restitution of the price? If the good has remained intact, then he is obliged to inform the buyer and give him the option of rescinding the contract if he wishes to do so. Yet if there is no need to fear that the buyer will suffer any noticeable inconvenience, and if otherwise at the given price the good proves to be useful for the buyer, then the seller is not obliged to rescind the contract. He risks committing a mortal sin, though. But all in all he is not obliged, because he did not cause noticeable damage, even if he sinned. In this manner, the practice of those who sell Moselle wine as if it were Rhine wine can often be excused, as long as the just price is not exceeded. If the good has not remained intact, for example, because it has been consumed, and the buyer did not suffer any detriment, then the seller is not obliged, that is, provided that the just price has not been exceeded. If the price did exceed the just price, then contractual equality needs to be restored through amicable settlement.[5]

2.1.4. Remarks

***Obvious defects*—**I said that "the seller is obliged to reveal the defects of the goods that are most hidden," since he may consider the obvious defects to be easily detectable by the buyer. If he believes, however, that they are not detectable, then he is obliged to reveal the obvious defects too. For a buyer generally asks about all kind of defects.

90. *No liability for praising the merits of his good*—Even though a seller praises his good higher than it is really worth,

4. This is explicitly stated in Dig. 19.1.13.

5. See Lopez, *Instructorium conscientiae*, part. 2, cap. 42, and the other advocates of this opinion cited by him.

or conceals a defect that does not make it noticeably less useful for the purpose for which it is sought, neither is the contract to be deemed void nor is the seller obliged to make restitution. First of all, this is common practice among the merchants, and it is widely known among the buyers. Furthermore, it does not cause the buyers any noticeable harm. Finally, it would be far too harsh to demand that such a group of people observe so strict a rule as to reveal every single defect. This is especially true when the buyer does not pose any specific questions about possible defects but merely asks the seller to deliver him a product that is useful and of good quality.[6]

2.2. When the Buyer Relies on His Own Judgment

2.2.1. Principle

91. If the buyer relies on his own judgment and chooses a good at random without asking questions about anything other than the price, the seller is not committing a sin against justice, even though he does not reveal a hidden defect. He should only beware of selling above the just price and should adjust—that is, lower—the price according to the defects of the good. This is clearly stated by Divine Thomas, since he only requires the seller to reveal a defect that might make the buyer run a risk—and that he can still do after concluding the contract.[7]

This is proven by the fact that the seller is not committing any injustice in the contract itself, since he is selling his good at the just price. Furthermore, he is not enticing the buyer into the contract through unjust practices. For he is not causing the buyer to enter into the contract through either lying or fraud.

6. Such is the opinion of Lopez in the passage quoted, and of Victoria and other authors cited by him.

7. See Divine Thomas, *Summa Theologiae*, 2a2ae, quaest. 77, art. 3 and *Quaestiones quodlibeticae*, quodlib. 2, art. 10. This view is shared by Sotus, *De iustitia et iure*, lib. 6, quaest. 3, art. 2; St. Antoninus, *Summa Theologica*, part. 2, tit. 1, cap. 17, par. 6; Lopez and Victoria, at the place cited.

Consequently, in this case he is not committing any injustice. In sum, if there is no injustice either in the contract itself or in the way that the contract was entered into, there is absolutely no trace of injustice here.

2.2.2. Objections and Answers

The fact that he is not revealing the defect is not a valid counterargument, since the seller is not obliged as a matter of justice to do that. In fact, the task of investigating the goods falls on the buyer. Consequently, the buyer cannot recover the damage from a seller who did not reveal the defects. He should rather blame the deception on himself, because without asking the opinion of the seller he solely relied on his own judgment to buy the good.

The second counterargument is inappropriate, too. It consists of the Roman maxim, found in Digest 19.1.13 and 21.1.1, that "a seller should reveal all hidden defects to the buyer, otherwise an *actio redhibitoria* will be granted." This maxim is not a valid counterargument, since it pertains to positive law, and, consequently, is only in force where it is received in practice. Alternatively, it needs to be understood in the case when the buyer explicitly asked questions, or in the sense that an action to rescission or restitution will only be given if decreed by the judge.

2.2.3. Remarks

92. It should be noted, first, that a seller who conceals defects by means of tricks cannot be excused, since his deceit causes the contract, as has been said before. The same holds true if he exhibits the defective good along with quality products, so that a buyer cannot possibly distinguish them from one another.

93. Second, even though not to inform a buyer relying on his own judgment does not go against justice, it may go against charity as, for example, when the seller notices that the buyer is deceived through naïveté, and when he thinks that the good might be useless for a particular buyer, though it may in fact be very useful for other buyers.

94. ***If the good is thought to be noxious***—If the good is thought to be noxious because of the hidden defect, then it seems like the seller is obliged to reveal the defect as a matter of justice too, at least after concluding the contract. This is the common opinion of the doctors. For by the mere fact that he is offering for sale a good with a hidden defect, the seller is obliged by virtue of his office to take care that nobody suffers from its noxiousness. Otherwise he seems to be the cause of the ensuing damage, as in the case of a wild horse, a sheep suffering from a disease, or defective building materials.[8] Nevertheless, I repeat that in my view the seller is not obliged to do this before the conclusion of the contract if the buyer is relying on his own judgment, as long as after concluding the contract the buyer can be warned about all the damages and inconveniences of the good.[9]

8. See Dig. 19.1.13.

9. See Sotus and Lopez, cited above.

QUESTION 12

WHEN A GOOD IS LOST OR DAMAGED, DOES THE LOSS FALL ON THE BUYER OR THE SELLER?

1. If It Is Lost after the Delivery, It Is the Buyer's Loss

95. The loss falls on the buyer when the sold good is lost or damaged after the delivery, even if the price has not been paid yet. This is because ownership has passed to the buyer after the delivery, and "the thing is lost to the owner."[1]

2. If a Designated Good Is Lost before Delivery, It Is the Buyer's Loss

96. If a specific and designated good (e.g., this horse, that house, or this jar of wine) is lost after the conclusion of the contract of sale and before the delivery, the loss falls on the buyer. Hence, the seller is under no obligation of making restitution of his price. In the same manner, a price increase is to the

---

1. See above, chapter 3, question 3; below, question 19.

advantage of the buyer.[2] This is because under *ius gentium*, the absolute conclusion of a contract of sale of a designated good is sufficient to transfer ownership. *Ius civile*, on the other hand, for certain reasons prescribes that ownership is not automatically transferred before delivery.[3] Yet it is not the intention of *ius civile* to stop all the conveniences and inconveniences that follow from a true transfer of ownership from falling on the buyer until the delivery takes place. And so, although it blocks ownership, it does not block its usual effects. This is right because it is the intention of the contracting parties that the good is passed to the buyer along with all its consequences, unless otherwise agreed. However, if the damage or loss is caused by the fault of the seller, who is responsible for the care of a good by virtue of his office until he hands it over to the buyer, the seller himself is liable. This also applies when the seller is in default with regard to the delivery and the damage or loss occurs in the meantime, unless the damage would have just as likely occurred in the hands of the buyer.[4]

3. If the Good Is Sold by Measure or Is Not Designated, It Is the Seller's Risk

97. The risk of the loss falls on the seller when the good is not designated (e.g., when you buy ten pecks of wheat from the harvest or the granary, or ten sheep from a flock) or when it is designated, but only by measure (e.g., the entire heap of wheat, for one florin per unit of measurement), before the transfer or measuring.[5] The reason is that there is assumed to be a tacit

---

2. As is expressly held in Dig. 18.1.35.5 and Cod. 4.48.1–6. See also Silvester, *Silvestrina summa*, part. 1, s.v. *Emptio*, num. 3; Covarruvias, *Variarum resolutionum*, lib. 3, cap. 3, num. 5.

3. Cf. above, chapter 3, question 3.

4. As Silvester, at the place cited, rightly points out.

5. This is expressly held by Dig. 18.1.35.1. See also Silvester, at the place cited above; Covarruvias, *Variarum resolutionum*, lib. 3, cap. 3, num. 7.

condition, namely, *if the good is transferred*, in the case of a sale of a good that is either not designated or only designated by measure.[6] Consequently, when no transfer or measuring (which in a sense encompasses a transfer, since it requires the buyer's presence) takes place, the buyer will not be liable, because the sale is not considered completed as long as this condition has not been fulfilled.

98. *Change in value in the meantime pertains to the buyer*— Note that if a good increases in value in the meantime, or decreases in value through no fault or delay of the seller, the buyer bears the advantages and disadvantages. This is because one buys a good as it will be at the time of the transfer, exposing oneself to fortuitous events.[7]

6. Dig. 18.1.35.1.

7. Silvester and Covarruvias, at the place cited.

Question 13

Can the Seller Reap the Fruits or Benefits from a Sold Good until the Price Is Paid?

1. Conflicting Opinions

99. Covarruvias confirms that fruits that come into existence after the sale are owed to the seller until the buyer pays.[1] If the good has already been transferred and the buyer reaps these fruits, he is obliged to compensate the seller, because they actually belong to him. This also applies in case the buyer is not in default, for instance when he has been granted a payment period. He bases this on *Curabit* (Cod. 4.49.5), a Roman law provision stating that "the Governor of a province shall compel the buyer to restore a part of the price along with the interests generated by reason of the perceived fruits and by favor of minority of age, if, after having obtained possession of a property, he has reaped the fruits, even if he was not in default." Covarruvias and other learned doctors understand "interests" to mean compensatory interests on the fruits that the seller should have reaped, and not lucrative interests, namely, usury, which is forbidden. Ulpian

1. Covarruvias, *Variarum resolutionum*, lib. 3, cap. 4, num. 1 and following.

states that "it is most equitable that the buyer should pay interests on the price since he enjoys the fruits of the good."[2]

However, Petrus de Navarra refutes this opinion as completely objectionable.[3]

2. Preliminary Distinctions

To solve this debate, it should be noted that we can distinguish between fruits existing at the time of the contract and fruits that come into existence afterward.

2.1. Hanging Fruits

100. As to hanging fruits, that is, fruits not yet separated from their object, it is certain that the value they have at that time is owed to the buyer, unless otherwise agreed upon.[4] This is because fruits actually existing at the time of the contract and attached to their object are deemed to be part of the purchased good. Accordingly, they are bought along with the good at the price agreed upon. For that reason, they are owed to the buyer as soon as he has paid the price, as is the good itself. I said "the value they have at that time" because the fruits are not considered to be part of the purchased good if the added value due to growth were taken into account. For instance, when you buy a vineyard when it is in bloom, the value of the flowers belongs to you as a part of the purchased good. This is not the case with the increase they acquire due to growth, because it is a consequence and the fruit of the purchased good, not a part of it.

---

2. Dig. 19.1.13.20.

3. Petrus de Navarra, *De ablatorum restitutione in foro conscientiae*, lib. 3, cap. 2, num. 157; Silvester, *Silvestrina summa*, part. 2, s.v. *Usura* 2, quaest. 11 and many others.

4. Explicitly in Dig. 19.1.13.10. This is common doctrine as shown by Gomezius, *Commentaria variaeque resolutiones iuris civilis, communis, et regii*, tom. 2, cap. 2, num. 11; and Covarruvias, *Variarum resolutionum*, lib. 1, cap. 15, num. 1.

2.2. Fruits Originating after the Time of the Contract, When the Buyer Has Offered the Price and the Seller Is in Default

101. As to fruits that come into existence after the time of the contract, or as to later increase, we have to make a distinction. For either the buyer has paid the price, or at least made an offer, or he did not. If he paid the price or made an offer to the seller who fails to deliver the good, then all those fruits are owed to the buyer. What is more, the seller is obliged to pay every intrinsic interest, as when the buyer would have derived more profit from the good (i.e., when the good has been damaged or has lost value while it remained in the seller's possession, whereas the buyer, if he had already possessed the good, could have used the opportunity to sell it for a profit, or at least the good would not have been damaged if delivered to him). The reason behind this is that the seller is the cause of this loss on account of the unjustified detention of the good.

102. I said "every intrinsic interest" because the seller does not owe the buyer any extrinsic interest (i.e., interest for something that happens to the buyer by accident) that may arise from, for instance, the fact that he could not transfer the good to a location where its value could increase, or the fact that his slaves have starved to death because the goods were not delivered.[5] Conversely, if the buyer fails to pay the price, he is only liable to pay interest on the price to the seller. He is not, however, obliged to pay interest on forgone profits on account of the fact that the seller could not make profits with the price.[6]

It should be noted that this is all to be understood as applying to the external court. Because in the court of conscience, there is no distinction between intrinsic and extrinsic interest or between interest on interest and interest on foregone profits. For

---

5. Explicitly in Dig. 19.1.21.3.

6. Explicitly in Dig. 18.6.20.

all those causing damage wrongfully are liable to pay all interest that could have been foreseen with probability.[7]

2.3. Fruits Originating after the Time of the Contract, When the Buyer Has Made No Offer and the Seller Did Not Give Him Credit

103. When the buyer did not pay or made no offer and the seller does not give him credit, then these fruits are owed to the seller under imperial Roman law. So if the good has been delivered to the buyer, who then reaps its fruits, the buyer is obliged under the same law to pay interest on the price in relation to the fruits.[8] This is the case when, for example, you have sold your house straightforwardly for 1,000 guilders and the buyer does not pay after concluding the contract even though you had not granted him a payment period, or when he maintained that he was planning on paying promptly, yet he does not. The first reason for this is that in this case ownership has not been transferred yet, even if the good has been delivered, which happened through the buyer's fault.[9] Consequently, the fruits deservedly go to the seller, who has kept ownership by operation of law. The second reason is that equity does not allow a buyer to reap the fruits from a purchased good while the seller is not able to benefit from the price (although he wants to) due to the buyer's fault.[10]

104. ***Compensatory and lucrative interests***—A possible objection would be that interests are forbidden. Covarruvias responds that lucrative interests are forbidden but compensatory interests are not,[11] because the latter compensates the fruits that were

7. As the theologians commonly teach and as follows from the above, chapter 7, questions 6 and 8, and chapter 20, questions 11 and 12.

8. Gomezius and Covarruvias, cited above, and as can be gleaned from the cited laws.

9. Inst. 2.1, § *Venditae*.

10. As can be gleaned from Dig. 19.1.13.

11. Covarruvias, *Variarum resolutionum*, lib. 3, cap. 4, num. 1.

owed to the seller. For the buyer does not pay interests as if the price had been lent to him, but because he derives fruits from it that still belong to the seller. Consequently, if the buyer does not reap any fruits and the seller would not have reaped any fruits as well, then the buyer is not liable to pay any interest. If he benefits a lot, he is liable to pay a lot of interest, namely, an amount equal to the number of fruits obtained. For example, you have bought a house for 1000 guilders, which yields 50 guilders if you rent it out. If you have not paid the price and move into the house or rent it out, you are obliged to entirely compensate the seller for the use of the house (because that is its fruit) and consequently pay 50 guilders. If you have only paid half of the price, then you are obliged to pay half of the value of the fruits (i.e., 25 guilders). If you have paid a third of the price, you are obliged to pay two thirds of the value of the fruits, and so forth, maintaining the proportion between the parts of the price of the fruits that must be paid for and the parts of the price itself that are still to be paid.

2.4. Fruits Originating after the Time of the Contract, When the Seller Has Delivered the Good and Granted a Delay

105. When the seller has delivered the good to the buyer, having given credit to the latter and granted a delay for payment, all fruits are owed to the buyer, who is not liable to pay interest on the price not yet paid.[12] This is because the seller is thought to renounce the imperial provision in the law *Curabit* when he delivers the good of his own accord and allows for a delay without any other agreement.[13]

Yet it should be noted that in this case, according to Covarruvias and many legal experts he cites, the seller can stipulate interests until the price is paid. Their reasoning is that the seller could have kept the fruits for himself if he had not wanted to deliver

12. Covarruvias, cited above, num. 5.

13. Cod. 4.49.5.

the good and give credit to the buyer. In addition, he could have demanded interests on the price if he had delivered the good and had not been willing to give credit to the buyer.[14] Now, due to the fact that he delivers the good to the buyer and gives him credit, the seller does not burden the buyer, but rather does him a service and gives him an advantage. For this reason the seller does not lose the right to demand interests on the price in relation to the fruits until the price has been paid.

106. ***Corollaries***—From Covarruvias's opinion it follows, first, that if I sell you a house for 1000 guilders, giving credit and delivering the house to you, then I am allowed to stipulate that you pay the price of the rent until you have paid me the price of the house.

107. Second, if I sell it to you without giving credit and I deliver it to you, you will be obliged to pay interests on the price by operation of law, even if that was not part of the agreement, since you are considered to be in default.

108. Third, if I sell you a house for 1000 guilders, I can stipulate that I reap the fruits of the rent until another fruit-yielding good has been found that can be purchased with the price. In the meantime, that price will be left in a deposit or with the buyer, according to the buyer's wishes. For I can sell under the condition that no delivery can take place before another fruit-yielding good has been found that can be purchased with the price. When that contract has been entered into, I can add another contract in which I make the delivery and in which I transfer ownership of the house along with the right to reap its fruits until the other good has been found, in exchange for an annual installment that is equivalent to the fruits.[15]

It should be noted that what has been said about the third and fourth assertion in sections 103 through 105, about the consequences concerning the fruits the seller reaps and the interests

14. Cod. 4.49.5.

15. Molina, *De iustitia et iure*, tom. 2, disput. 368.

the buyer pays in sections 106 through 108, all goes according to imperial Roman law.

3. The Solution That Is More True

The view contrary to imperial Roman law, however, is more true and more in line with natural equity, namely, that all fruits belong to the buyer once the sale has been concluded, unless explicitly agreed upon otherwise. If it is agreed upon that they remain at the seller's disposal for a given time, then the risk has to fall upon the seller as well. Then, when he fails to pay, the buyer is only liable to pay interest.[16]

109. This opinion is common among the theologians and can be proven in the following manner.

First, once the contract is concluded, the good is considered to instantly belong to the buyer, so that when the good is lost, it is lost to the buyer, not the seller, as I have said above in question 12 about goods sold not by measure, but by body (i.e., as the body of the good is presented to our senses). Now it is not according to equity that the risk falls solely on the buyer, while in the meantime the seller reaps all the fruits. There would be no equality of condition among the contracting parties. The seller would only reap the benefits of the sale and would not be obliged to bear any risk or disadvantage, which would completely fall on the buyer. This is the reason why the seller, if he wishes to benefit from the fruits, also has to bear the risk during that entire period.

110. Second, such a contract seems to be implicitly usurious, as the seller appears to reap the fruits due to the delay in the payment of the price. He neither reaps the fruits because of potential profits foregone, as Covarruvias admits (otherwise, if

---

16. Silvester, *Silvestrina summa*, part. 2, s.v. *Usura* 2, quaest. 11, citing for this opinion Franciscus Mayronius, Bernardinus Senensis, Rosella, and Archidiaconus in 4. dist. 15. The theologians share the same view, as Archidiaconus shows.

no profit were foregone to his detriment, he would not be allowed to benefit, which Covarruvias, however, denies), nor because of some risk he bears, since all risk falls on the buyer. Consequently, he benefits because of the delay in payment.

Third, the seller's interest is either harmed because of the delay in payment, or it is not. If his interest is harmed, he can provide for that by adding a clause to the contract from the start and in doing so sufficiently cover himself. If his interest is not harmed, then it is not equitable that he demands the fruits or their compensation while having the risk fall on the buyer. Likewise, if the buyer is in default of payment and the seller's interest suffers harm from that, the latter is given plenty of satisfaction if the interest is estimated. This is why there is no reason for the seller to reap any fruits if he does not want to bear any risk at the same time and has stipulated this in the contract from the start.

4. Refutation of Covarruvias

111. As to the law *Curabit*, one can respond that it has been abolished by canon law to the extent that it allows for interests. Therefore, we must have recourse to natural equity, so that the buyer is obliged to compensate for the harm, either when he is in default or when it has been stipulated in the contract. The same goes for the law *Iulianus* (Dig. 19.1.13) because all these laws talk of interests on a price in absolute terms, whether the fruits are big or small. Yet the rate of interest was set at 6 percent per year under imperial law.[17] What Covarruvias teaches based on Carolus Molinaeus, namely, that those laws deal with compensatory interests on fruits, does not seem to be true for three reasons:

1. Fruits in reality belong to the buyer, especially in the case of the law *Curabit*, in which the buyer was not in default.

17. Cod. 4.32.26.

2. Otherwise the laws would not state that interest has to be paid on the price, but that the fruits have to be compensated or that they belong to the seller.
3. Otherwise the same interest would not always have to be paid.

112. You will object that it is most equitable that the buyer pays interest on the price because he has the use and enjoyment of the good.[18] In response, I say that it is not equitable unless the seller takes on an equal amount of disadvantage because of the price delay, or unless he bears the risk of the good, the value of the fruits is on a par with the interest, and this is all stipulated in the contract from the start. For if the seller takes on the risk, he can have the contract state that the fruits are his until the price is paid, and he can accordingly let the buyer have them in exchange for a certain installment, which can be qualified as interest.

18. Dig. 19.1.13, see above.

Question 14

Is It Lawful to Add a Buyback or Sellback Clause to a Contract of Sale?

1. Response

113. It is licit as long as it happens at a just price. It is certainly common doctrine that a sale with a buyback clause in favor of the seller is licit. This is also obvious in annuity contracts, which almost always come with this provision, at least implicitly, since this clause is understood to be part of those contracts by operation of law. The same is confirmed by Leviticus 25, where the Lord wants the sons of Israel to be able to buy back all their sold possessions, except for the houses built inside the city. This is because everyone is arbiter of their own goods and they can impose modalities on those goods as they please. The question concerning a purchase with a provision of a sellback clause in favor of the buyer is more difficult. Nevertheless, it is more true that it is not illicit, as long as it happens at a just price.[1] The reason

1. Covarruvias, *Variarum resolutionum*, lib. 3, cap. 9, num. 3, where he cites Ioannes Medina (*q. de censu redimibilli, ult. De Usurea* in favor of this view), along with John Major in 4.d.15.quaest.34, and Imolensis and Alexander.

behind this is that, just as the burden that the seller places on the buyer can be compensated by a just price (i.e., by subtracting an equal amount from the price), so too can the burden that the buyer places on the seller be compensated by raising the price an equal amount in the first sale. Yet, how do we know whether the price is just?

2. Determination of the Just Price

2.1. Buyback Clause in Favor of the Seller

2.1.1. The Good Has to Be Sold Cheaper

114. When a good is sold with the buyback provision in favor of the seller only (i.e., that he is able to buy back the good if he wishes), it has to be sold cheaper than its bare value. This is because the seller imposes on the buyer a burden that is estimable in money, namely, the fact that the buyer is obliged to sell him back the good if the seller so wishes, or that he has to make restitution within a certain timeframe. Therefore, we must subtract the value of the burden from the price.[2]

2.1.2. Remarks

115. ***Buying back at the same price***—Please note, first of all, that it is not inequitable that the seller sells with the provision to repurchase at the same price, for this is just the same as a contract of sale with the provision that allows you to dissolve the contract after a certain period of time. In fact, the repurchase does not constitute a new contract, but only the dissolution of the previous one on grounds of the provision. This is why the seller does not have to pay the amount that the good is worth at that moment in time, because at that moment no new contract comes into being. Likewise, it is not inequitable that the seller sells for a certain period under the condition that the good returns to him at the end of the period without payment. If the seller

2. As Major rightly points out in the source above, q.34, at the end.

wants to buy back his goods before the end of the period, the buyer is obliged to include in the sum the fruits he reaped over the years pro rata. This is the way the Jews sold their belongings, as Leviticus 25 makes clear.

Yet, in the event that the seller wants to reserve the right to repurchase, the buyer who has bought the good at a just price could demand from him that he pays the value of the good at the moment he wishes to repurchase. Consequently, if the good was probably going to increase in value by the time of repurchase, or if the buyer was planning on selling the good to a third party at a bigger profit, then the buyer can demand a higher price than the seller had originally received for it. The reason for this is that the buyer does not have to agree to the provision that dissolves the sale, but he can demand that the seller buys back the good through a new contract when he wishes to recuperate his good and, as a consequence, at the price it is worth then. It is quite important, then, what kind of contract you enter into. Indeed, even if the good was not going to increase in value, the buyer could still demand more than he had given, because he has bought the good with a burden in favor of the seller. Accordingly, he had to pay less for the good than if he had bought it without the burden. Yet, he is forced to sell it back unburdened, which is why he can demand a price that he sets by himself and that is higher than the price of a burdened good.

116. ***Inequitable practices***—It should be noted, second, that it would be inequitable to sell with a buyback clause at the same price if the buyer would have to suffer big expenses for the good and would reap little fruit in return, so that the fruits do not compensate the burden of the expenses and the bearing of the risk. Equality is not observed in that case because the buyer has to restore more than he has received. It would be equally inequitable if the contract stipulated that the seller can repurchase at a lower price than he originally sold it for, unless, perhaps, when it is undisputed that the good will decrease in value.

2.2. Buyback Clause in Favor of the Buyer

2.2.1 The Good Has to Be Bought Dearer

117. When a buyback clause is added to a contract of sale solely in favor of the buyer (i.e., that the seller is obliged to buy the good back, if the buyer wishes), then the buyer has to buy the good at a higher price than it is worth and, accordingly, than he could sell it to a third party. This is because such a buyer acquires the good forever as far as he is concerned, just as every other person who would buy a good without an additional clause. Yet he imposes a burden on the seller to a greater extent, which is why he has to make compensation, since the burden is estimable in the price.

2.2.2. Can the Buyer Impose a Buyback Clause at the Same Price?

118. It would seem that it is not possible for the buyer to stipulate that the seller is obliged to repurchase at the same price. The reason is that he cannot sell it to a third party at that price, as I have said, since the good is not worth so much on its own as it is in combination with the burden imposed on the seller. Hence, the seller cannot be obliged to repurchase at the same price.

This is confirmed, first, by the following example: You have a house with an estimated value of 4,000 guilders. I buy your house for 4,300 with the provision that you are obliged to buy it back from me if I so desire after a couple of years. So I pay 4,000 for the house that I completely acquire for myself, along with 300 for the burden I impose on you. For it is very burdensome for the seller to always have money at the ready or via friends so as to repurchase the house when the buyer so pleases. Indeed the seller has already undergone this burden by buying back the house, and so the buyer cannot claim back the price he paid for that burden. Moreover, it is not possible from the start to agree that this price be given back; only the price of the house can be given back (i.e., 4,000).

This is confirmed, second, by the following argument. If I bought a house through a simple contract of sale without that clause, I assume that I would have to pay 4000 guilders. Now, if after concluding that contract I wanted to enter into an agreement with the seller so as to make him obliged to buy it back at the same price (i.e., 4,000), I assume that I would have to give him 300 guilders for that obligation, and I would not be able to reclaim those 300 guilders later when he buys it back. Consequently, this cannot be allowed in the other contract, either, where the buyback clause was included from the start. For agreements that are unjust when they are entered into separately, cannot be just when they are entered into jointly, either.

Following a strict interpretation of the law, it would seem that such a clause is inequitable, as the aforementioned reasons prove. Yet, considering people's common use and estimation, I think it can be excused. In fact, people attach great importance to the fact that the buyer is deprived for such a long time of the 300 guilders he gave in return for that burden, and that perhaps the house will never be bought back, and that in the meantime the seller can use that money to his own advantage in the hope that he will never be forced to repurchase. All these things can often be estimated to be of equal value as the burden the seller imposed upon himself. In that case, the buyer could stipulate that the seller repurchase at the same price, not through a new contract, but through a bare dissolution of the contract, as often happens with annuities.

2.2.3. A Buyback Clause at a Higher Price and the Presumption of Usury

119. If the buyer stipulates that the seller has to buy back the good sold at a higher price after several years, the contract will be invalid (unless there are excuses, such as the amelioration of the good or a future increase in price), because equality is not observed as to the price. However, there will be no usury, but there will arise only a suspicion of usury, especially if the fruits reaped are included in the principal sum. Hence, a contract such as the following is presumed *de jure* to be usurious: Someone buys a farm for 23 pounds from someone who needs money, on the condition that if the buyer is not satisfied with the purchase within two years the seller is obliged to buy it back for 26 pounds (which includes the fruits) within one year starting from the notice of discontent.

***Canon* Illo vos**—This presumption *de jure* stems from three indications taken together, as appears from canon *Illo vos* (*Dec. Greg.* 3.21.4). First, that the fruits are included in the principal, which does not usually happen when a good has really been sold, because they belong to the buyer from then on. So this is a sign that there has not been a real sale, but a transfer of a thing pledged to secure a loan. Second, that he demands three pounds more than he gave. Third, that the specific buyer in the case has repeatedly been involved in usurious practices. Accordingly, when all these three signs come together at the same time, we need to qualify it as a usurious contract in the external court. I will discuss in chapter 22, question 10 whether such a clause in favor of the buyer is licit with regard to annuities.

2.3. Buyback Clause in Favor of Both Parties

120. When the clause is added to the contract of sale in favor of both parties in a way that the seller has the option to repurchase and the buyer to resell when they so please, then the good has to be sold at a lower price than it is actually worth, but at a higher price than if it were sold with a buyback clause solely in favor of the seller. So if the good is worth 100, it would be worth 80 in case of a clause solely in favor of the seller. Yet it might be worth 88 or 90 when the clause is in favor of both parties, according to the judgment of a prudent man and considering all the circumstances.[3]

3. Medina, in his last question on usury.

3. Remarks

3.1. Limitation

It should first be noted that all of the above must be understood without taking into account the damage to the interests of the buyer and seller. For if the interests of the buyer are damaged by reason of the purchase, he will be able to pay less for the good and stipulate that it can only be bought back after a certain period of time, so as to compensate the loss in profit with the fruits. He can also stipulate that the seller buy back at the same price.

3.2. Whether a Legal Action Against the Thing (*actio in rem*) Is Given on the Grounds of This Clause

121. Second, it should be noted that, although it may be assumed[4] that the sellback clause gives the seller recourse to legal action against the thing and that he can accordingly claim back the good wherever it is situated, it does seem that the opposite holds true, that is, that the seller only has recourse to legal action on the facts of the case (*actio in factum*) or against the person (*actio in personam*). So when the buyer sells and delivers to a third party the house he has bought with such a provision, you will not be able to take back that house from the third party. You can, however, bring a suit against the person who sold it to make reparations for all damage incurred.[5] The reason is that such a clause does not give you more power or more right than a simple sale agreement. A simple sale agreement without delivery does not give you any real right (*ius in rem*) but only a personal right

4. Covarruvias, *Variarum resolutionum*, lib. 3, cap. 8, num. 2 and 3.

5. Alexander, Iason, Curtius, and others cited in Covarruvias and Gomezius, *Commentaria variaeque resolutiones iuris civilis, communis, et regii*, tom. 2, cap. 2, num. 29; and Molina, *De iustitia et iure*, tom. 2, disput. 374.

(*ius in personam*), and so neither does this clause.[6] But more on that below in question 19.

3.3. No Liability for Eviction

Third, it should be noted that when the seller repurchases a good he once sold with a buyback provision, the party from whom he buys it back is not liable for eviction as if the seller were under a sale agreement. For the repurchase is not a purchase, but the termination or dissolution of a previous contract. The repurchase happens by virtue of the first contract, under which the seller sold with such a provision. This is why the consent of the other party is not needed, and it can take place against his will. Also, no sales tax is due.

6. See above, chapter 3, question 3.

Question 15

To Whom Belong the Fruits Generated in the Meantime When the Contract of Sale Is Dissolved?

122. I assume a contract can be dissolved in five ways:[1]

1. By a New Agreement

When you are dissatisfied with the contract after its conclusion and after a just period of time, you can rescind the agreement by mutual assent of the parties to the contract. Then you can enter into a new contract of sale and change the price or keep it the same. In that case, all the fruits produced by the good during the first contract period belong to the first buyer, according to what I said in question 13, because the risk falls on him.

The same holds true if the contract is terminated by the remedy of law *Secunda* (Cod. 4.44.2), that is, when the seller has been deceived for more than half of the just price, and the buyer does not want to pay extra but rather wants to dissolve the contract. For both the hanging and future fruits belong to the buyer in accordance with the value they have at the time of

1. For much more on this, see Gomezius, *Commentaria variaeque resolutiones iuris civilis, communis, et regii*, tom. 2, cap. 2, num. 21 and following.

the rescission.[2] The reason for this is that even though the just price has not been paid, the sale is still valid and sufficient to transfer ownership once the delivery has taken place. This way he reaps the fruits of his own good, while those still hanging on it belong to him as well. This is confirmed by the fact that he has harmed the seller not by possessing the good or reaping its fruits, but by not paying the just price. Hence, he is only liable in the court of conscience for the amount that was of interest to the seller (i.e., the supplement to the price that had to be paid from the start). This is why the buyer owes nothing if all has taken place in good faith.

2. By a Sellback Clause Included in the First Contract of Sale

123. In this case, if the good has to be bought back at the same price, all fruits produced from the moment of the sale up to the moment of repurchase belong to the buyer in accordance with the value they have at that time, unless explicitly or tacitly otherwise agreed upon.[3] They belong to the first seller, however, who is entitled to restitution of the good, in accordance with the value the fruits acquire after the time of repurchasing or once the buyer is in default because he does not want to buy it back.

However, if there must be a different repurchase price, namely, the price that is current at the time of repurchase, then all hanging fruits belong to the first seller, who buys back the good, just as with all sales. The reason is that this qualifies as a new contract of sale, so the reseller can raise the price by reason of the hanging fruits. When the price does not change, there is no new contract, but only the rescission of an earlier one, which is why the price cannot be raised and no compensation for the

2. As Gomezius teaches in the source above, num. 24

3. Covarruvias, *Variarum resolutionum*, lib. 1, cap. 15, num. 6 and 7 along with many other doctors.

fruits can be claimed. Anyhow, it runs counter to equity if you are obliged to restore goods along with their fruits when you acquired those goods without any fruits.[4]

3. By *lex commissoria*

124. A sale is said to be dissolved by *lex commissoria* when something is sold under the condition that the buyer has to pay the price within a certain period of time or else the good is not sold and the contract is void. The buyer cannot pay the price any time after that period. At that very moment when the period ends, the contract is void automatically, but only if the seller so wishes, because the clause was included in his favor. That is why this condition is tacitly presumed.[5]

With regard to this third mode of dissolving a contract, all fruits belong to the seller if the clause has been stated with direct words (i.e., it was indicated that the contract would be considered void from the outset, or that the good would be considered not purchased). The reason for this is that even though the contract is pure or absolute (i.e., unconditional), and it has passed ownership onto the buyer (if delivery has taken place[6]), the contract is still terminated by that clause as if the contract never had existed. And all fruits must be restored accordingly. For even though the sale was not dependent on any condition, its effects were (namely, the ownership of the good and the transfer of the fruits onto the buyer) in a way that the contract completely dies away, as if it had never existed, if the condition is not met. In fact, it is treated as void from the outset with retroactive effect.

4. See Covarruvias, cited above; Molina, *De iustitia et iure*, tom. 2, disput. 374.

5. As can clearly be gleaned from Dig. 18.3.2 and 3.

6. As is taught by Gomezius, *Commentaria variaeque resolutiones iuris civilis, communis, et regii*, tom. 2, cap. 2, num. 30; and Covarruvias, *Variarum resolutionum*, lib. 3, cap. 8, num. 1.

However, if the clause has been stated obliquely or with indirect words (i.e., it was indicated that the contract will have to be rescinded in the future, or that the good will have to be returned to the seller), then all fruits produced during the contract belong to the buyer. The reason for this is that now the contract is not considered to be void retroactively from the conclusion of the contract, but only in the future. Hence, the fruits from before stay with the buyer. For all that, we do not have to take into consideration the form of the words, which is always ambiguous, as much as the intent of the contracting parties, at least in the court of conscience.

4. By *addictio in diem*

125. A contract of sale is said to be rescinded by *addictio in diem* when a good has been sold to someone under the condition that the good is not bought if someone else offers the seller better conditions within a certain time (e.g., within a month or a year). Instances of better conditions are a higher price and a more convenient or less burdensome way of obtaining payment.[7] In this case, what has been said in the third case applies, because the reasoning is the same for both.[8]

126. ***How the seller regains ownership***—First, it should be noted that both in the case of *lex commissoria* and *addictio in diem* the seller regains ownership even before the good has been returned by the buyer, if the clause has been expressed with direct words. If it has been stated obliquely, however, he only regains it after delivery, according to common doctrine. However, it is probable that in the fourth case, that is, in the case of *addictio in diem*, ownership is transferred before delivery, even if the clause was stated in oblique wording.[9]

---

7. Covarruvias, cited above, and as is made clear by Dig. 18.2.1 and 4.
8. See Covarruvias on this.
9. As Covarruvias teaches in the place cited above.

127. ***Taxes***—Second, it should be noted that in neither of the cases is the usual sales tax due, if the clause was stated with direct words. The reason is that the contract is terminated by the clause, as if it had never existed. For it is treated as void from the outset with retroactive effect. It does not matter that the sale was absolute and unconditional, because the right of ownership and every other right acquired from that sale were in a sense dependent on a condition and future event. The tax is due, however, when the clause was stated obliquely, because then the nullity is not retroactive, but is in the future. Hence, the contract remains in force until the moment it is void. Consequently, the prince derives a right to tax from that sale, just as he derives the right to tax from a sale rescinded by a sellback clause.[10]

5. By a Conditional Contract of Sale

128. If the sale was made under a condition, and the condition is not fulfilled, the sale is void. In this case, all fruits reaped before the condition is fulfilled belong to the seller. It does not matter that the good has already been delivered and the price paid, because the sale was not completed (for the completion and fulfillment depended on the condition), so that the delivery does not have the force to transfer the absolute right of ownership of the goods or fruits onto the buyer. I say "absolute" right, because it does transfer some amount of ownership and right over the good.[11] Yet, that entirely depends on the fulfillment of the condition, the lack of which makes an end to the agreement, as if it had never existed. However, if the buyer suffers loss of profit due to the payment of the price, he can stipulate the estimation

10. See Gomezius, *Commentaria variaeque resolutiones iuris civilis, communis, et regii*, tom. 2, cap. 2, num. 31, where he handles this clearly and elaborately.

11. As can be gleaned from Dig. 46.3.16. The doctors note the same there, along with Bartolus.

of this loss from the outset, so as to be compensated when the condition is not fulfilled.

If the condition is fulfilled, then all the fruits belong to the buyer, along with the good itself. The reason is that it is the nature of a conditional contract that the fulfillment of the condition has a retroactive effect on the contract, as though the contract had been completely concluded and the condition had been present from the start.[12]

Potestative conditions—Things are different when the condition is potestative, as the jurists call it (i.e., when its fulfillment lies solely within the power of the debtor). This condition has no retroactive effect, that is, unless another intent of the contracting parties is shown. Certainly in the court of conscience this intent has to be taken into special consideration.[13]

---

12. See above, chapter 21, question 1; Gomezius, *Commentaria variaeque resolutiones iuris civilis, communis, et regii*, tom. 2, cap. 2, num. 30, based on many laws, and at length in work cited, tom. 2, cap. 11, num. 30

13. Gomezius, at the place cited.

Question 16

Is the Mutual Sale-Purchase of the Same Good at a Different Price, a Practice Known by the Spaniards as *Baratas-Mohatras*, Licit?

129. For example, person A asks merchant B to lend him 100 guilders. B refuses to do so but proposes A the following twofold contract: B sells A merchandise on credit at the highest just price, say 105 or 106 guilders, in such a way that A becomes the owner and is free to sell it to anyone for ready money. In a *baratas-mohatras*, A offers the merchandise for sale to person B himself, who buys it back in exchange for ready money but at a lower price, namely, the medium or lowest just price, say 100 guilders. In this manner, A still owes B a total of 105 guilders.

130. Some doctors contend that this practice is unjust and is applied to cloak usury if the buyer is the same person as the original seller.

Yet it is truer that even in that case it is not unjust, as long as the limits of the just price are not exceeded. Consequently, in the credit sale the rigorous just price is the maximum and in the repurchase the lowest just price is the minimum.[1]

1. Such is the view of Navarrus, *Manuale*, lib. 3, num. 91; Petrus de Navarra, *De ablatorum restitutione in foro conscientiae*, lib. 3, cap. 2, num. 170; and more recent authors.

The reason for this is that the contract consists of two sales, each of which is perfectly just: the first sale is executed at the just price, however rigorous it may be, as is the resale of the same merchandise. It is irrelevant that the resale is executed at the minimum price, first, because the lowest just price is a just price anyway, especially if payment is made in ready money, and, second, because goods brought to the market on proposal of the seller decrease in value. It is also irrelevant that the buyer in the resale is actually the seller in the first agreement, for if everyone is allowed to buy at the lowest price, why not the original seller? In point of fact, he is doing a service to the other party, since the latter is freed from the concern to look for a buyer or an expensive broker. However, B is not allowed to force A to take him as a buyer, but rather must allow him to sell his good to the person of his choice.

131. ***It often goes against charity***—It should be noted, however, that this kind of contract is not entirely free of fault for the merchant who deliberately sells on credit in order to be able to repurchase the good at a minimum price. First, he might sin against charity when he forces a poor man to incur considerable costs to buy commodities that are of no use to him when actually he could easily have lent him money without experiencing any inconveniences from it. Second, he might sin by setting a bad example, since in the end the contract smells of evil and usury. Third, he might sin by bringing himself and his colleagues into disrepute.

132. He is not obliged to make restitution, according to Navarrus, at least not as a matter of justice. Indeed, he might well be obliged as a matter of charity, as when the other party is poor and is severely harmed by the contract. Since person B is causing the severe inconvenience suffered by A, he is obliged to remove it as a matter of charity as long as he can do so without suffering inconvenience himself. If, however, A is no longer poor, B is obliged neither by justice nor by charity anymore, and should he have sold in good faith without having considered a repurchase originally, but only because he was being asked to do so in ready money afterward, then he did not commit a sin.[2] The same holds true in the case when he has a good reason to conclude such a contract with a rich person, provided there is no scandal.

2. As is correctly taught by Angelus Carletus a Clavasio, *Summa Angelica*, part. 2, s.v. *Usura* 1, num. 60.

QUESTION 17

CAN YOU SELL ANOTHER'S PROPERTY AND KEEP THE PRICE?

We have briefly touched on this subject in chapter 14, questions 1 and 5, and in chapter 20, question 18, paragraph 163. Note that a distinction has to be made between selling in good faith (i.e., not knowing the good belongs to someone else), and selling in bad faith. Moreover, there is also the question whether or not the seller has enriched himself.

1. When He Sold in Good Faith

133. When he sold in good faith and did not enrich himself, he is not obliged to make restitution of the price to the owner. This is proven by the fact that he is not obliged to make restitution either by virtue of the thing received or by virtue of unjust receiving. He is not obliged to the owner on the grounds of the thing received since he no longer possesses the thing and he did not derive any advantage from it. He is also not obliged to the owner on the grounds of unjust receiving since he did not commit any injustice. He is not even obliged to make restitution to the buyer, as long as the buyer keeps the good, since the contract was valid and the buyer has not suffered any damage from it.

However, when a third party claims ownership of the good or when it is restored to the owner, the seller is liable for eviction.

The seller is not obliged to point out to the buyer that the good is someone else's property, if the seller by chance comes to find that out after conclusion of the sale contract. The reason is that the seller is not obliged to make sure at his own expense that a good is restored when that good belongs to another person and is alienated or lost through no fault of his own.[1]

2. When He Has Enriched Himself

134. If the seller is enriched by the sale, he has to restore that profit to the owner, because the profit replaces the owner's good. Even though the profit does not belong to the owner, still it is the product of the owner's good and it takes the place of that good. Therefore, the profit has to be restored, as if it were the fruits of the good. It is not appropriate that someone enriches himself with another's good without his own industry. Things are different when the profit is derived from his own industry as, for example, when he transported the good to a place where he could sell it with more profit. In that case, the seller will not be liable to make restitution, because the profit is the fruits of his own labor.[2]

3. When He Sold in Bad Faith

135. When the seller sold in bad faith and did not enrich himself, because he bought at the same price, a distinction must be made. For either he was able to restore the good to the owner, or he was not.

---

1. See above, chapter 14, questions 1 and 5.
2. As shown above, chapter 14, questions 1 and 5.

3.1. When He Was Able to Restore the Good to the Owner

If he was able to restore it to its owner and he alienated the good, it is almost common doctrine that he is liable to restore the price or the estimated value of the thing. The reason is that he inflicts damage by alienating the good, as though he destroyed it. Moreover, he had no right to alienate it. Things are different when something is bought from a thief and returned to that thief, because this sale does not qualify as alienation or transfer, but as rescission of the previous contract. According to a probable opinion, he could do this to avoid the loss of the price, if he could not protect himself against the harm in any other manner.[3] Yet, except for this case, the seller in bad faith is obliged to restore the good to its owner, while losing the price. If he does not do so, he is obliged to compensate its value.

3.2. When He Was Not Able to Restore the Good to the Owner

But if he was not able to restore the good to its owner and by alienating it he did not make it any more difficult to recover it, he does not seem to be liable to make restitution, except to the extent he has been enriched by that alienation. The reason for this is that he has not caused any harm to the owner with that alienation. So he is not liable either on grounds of the thing received or on grounds of unjust receiving. Of course, this is all under the assumption that he did not steal the good from the owner and that he is not the cause behind the fact that restitution cannot be made to the owner. This opinion is confirmed by the fact that many doctors state on the same grounds that what has been bought from a thief, even in bad faith, can be restored to that thief to recover the price, even if the good could be restored to the rightful owner.[4] So there is all the more reason that the

---

3. See above, chapter 14, question 3.

4. As shown above in chapter 14, question 3.

seller is able to sell it to another person without causing any harm when the good cannot be restored to the rightful owner.

Those who sold goods of the church in England and Holland— This is also the reason why many in England and Holland who have bought ecclesiastical real estate from others and then later sold it to still others can be excused from restitution. For they caused the church no harm by these sales, because those goods cannot be restored in this state of affairs. Hence, they are not obliged to make restitution of the price or its equivalent to the church. If, however, they have been enriched with the fruits or the sale, they are liable to the extent of the enrichment. For the fruits belong to the church due to the sole fact that they stem from a good of the church, and the profit from the sale is owed to the church, even though the profit does not belong to the church, because the profit has in a way replaced the good, unless it stems from personal industry.

The seller is not liable vis-à-vis the buyer who bought the goods from him, because even though the contract was invalid and as a consequence ownership of the price was not transferred, he is not obliged to return the price to him, which he can keep instead of the good sold.[5] This is because the seller received and kept the price with the buyer's consent, while the buyer was not willing to terminate the contract and give back the purchased good. If, on the other hand, the buyer wanted to terminate the contract and give back what he bought, the seller should have given him back the price, because the contract had been void from the start.

---

5. See above, chapter 20, question 18.

Question 18

Is It Licit to Sell, Buy, and Keep Another's Property (e.g., a Good That Has Been Stolen)?

1. Provisional Answer

136. It would seem that such a thing can never be bought or kept for the following reasons: First, the seller is in no position to sell it, since he is a robber, a thief, or an unlawful detainer. Since the seller is obliged to return it to the owner, the buyer cannot buy it. Second, ownership is not transferred by such a sale (for the seller is not able to transfer onto another a right he does not have himself) and accordingly it specifically remains another's property. Moreover, another's property must be returned to the rightful owner, if possible. If it is not possible, however, because the rightful owner is unknown, it has to be given to the poor, since that is considered to be the owner's will. Thus, by giving it to the poor, the good is in a way returned to its rightful owner because fruits of the restitution return to the owner since the poor are praying for him, as the doctors teach. Third, those who buy stolen or plundered goods partake in the crime and in a way support the main authors of the crime, because if the latter could not find any buyers, they would not steal other people's commodities in the first place.

2. Response

In response to this provisional answer it should be noted that when another's good is sold by a thief, a robber, or some other unlawful possessor, either it is possible that it can be returned to its owner or it is not. In addition, either there can be hope that the owner will get it back, or that hope can be non-existent. Finally, either there will be many other buyers who will never give it back if I do not buy it first, or there will not be.

2.1. If There Was Hope of Recovery

If the owner has any hope of recovering his good in another way, then I cannot buy it, unless I have the intention of giving it back to him, in which case I cannot demand the price I paid for it, but only the reasonable amount the owner would have paid to get it back, after prudent consideration of all circumstances. The reason is that, since the good belongs to someone else and can be restored, it effectively has to be restored. Also, the owner cannot be obliged to pay anything, except to the extent that I managed his affairs in a useful manner, that is, for the estimated value of recovering the good. If I spent more, then I have to blame myself for my own imprudence because the owner is not obliged to pay for my errors.[1]

Objection—A possible objection is that the manager of affairs is only liable for gross negligence, since he manages everything for the sake of the utility of the other person. So the owner will be obliged to pay compensation, even if the negligence is of a lesser degree (e.g., I thought the good could not be recovered, or I paid more than was appropriate for buying back a good of such a kind).

Answer—I would say that he is not liable to the owner for slight negligence if it causes the owner harm (e.g., by spending the owner's money or by selling the good). However, if he causes

1. As can clearly be gleaned from Dig. 3.5.9.

himself harm by the management of another's affairs with like negligence (e.g., by spending his own money), then the owner is not liable to him, because he is only obliged to compensate the value that such prudent management or recovery of the good is estimated to be worth. So, if he paid too much of his own money by accident, he has to blame himself.

However, if the management was prudently set up under the circumstances, the owner is obliged to fully reimburse him, even if he was planning on recovering the good at a lower cost in some other way. For this happens by accident, and every owner could always use such an empty argument. The same applies even when the good happens to be lost or damaged afterward through no fault of the manager.[2]

2.2. If There Was No Hope of Recovery

If the owner has no likely hope that he will recover his good unless I buy it, and it can be restored if I buy it, then I cannot buy it with the intention of absolutely keeping it for myself. If I do that, the owner can claim it later without any compensation.

However, I can buy the good with the intention of showing it to him, so that he can either allow me to keep it or, if he does not, pay me just compensation for the management of his affairs.

The first part is considered right because the owner is not obliged to me to pay for the good, because it belongs to him (since no one is obliged to buy his own property), nor is he obliged to pay for the management of affairs (since I did not manage his affairs, but my own). For I did not buy the good to bring him any benefit, but to keep it myself. Hence, if the owner later on finds the good with the one who bought it from a thief for his own benefit, the owner will not be obliged to pay that person anything, except to the extent he has been enriched (e.g., when the good has been notably enhanced by the buyer's expenses).[3]

2. Dig. 3.5.9 (toward the end) and Dig. 3.5.21.

3. As can be clearly gleaned from Dig. 3.5.5.5.

If he did not know the good belonged to someone else— However, if he bought in good faith, not knowing that the good belonged to someone else, the owner would be obliged to reimburse his expenses, at least the amount he himself would have had to pay in order to recover the good.[4] For his affairs were managed in a useful manner, and it is not appropriate that the other person incurs this harm through no fault of his own.

The second part is considered right because when his affairs are managed so usefully, he is obliged to either reimburse the expenses[5] or let him have the thing bought, if he would rather be rid of the thing than reimburse the expenses. If he does not want to reimburse the expenses, the other person will nonetheless be able to hold him to some form of compensation, because it was with this intention that, at his own expense, he saved a good that would otherwise have been lost. This is common practice, provided that he did not redeem the good far below the limits of the just price. For if the good is worth far more than the expenses, and the owner does not want to reimburse the expenses and recover the good, then the manager of the owner's affairs has to be satisfied with the expenses, which he can either obtain through the authority of a judge or out of the good itself, if it yields fruits. He can also retain the good as if it were a pledge, until the owner pays for it.

2.3. If It Is Sold Publicly

137. When the owner has no likely hope that he can recover his good, and it is sold publicly, then I, too, can obviously buy it with the intention of either keeping it for myself or selling it if the owner does not appear, and with the intention of handing it over to him at the same price if he does appear. This can be proven because in this case the buyer does not harm the owner in any way. On the contrary, he manages the affairs of the owner

4. Dig. 3.5.30.

5. As is made clear in Dig. 3.5.1–3.

as much as he can. This is why the transfer of ownership with this burden is not considered to be against the owner's will, but according to his will.

Pirates' loot—In this way Catholics in Holland can buy commodities put up for sale publicly that heretics seized at sea. This is confirmed because otherwise all this profit would solely fall to the heretics while they are fomenting an unjust war and assaulting our religion. Nor do the heretics buy with the intention of giving back in the event the owner would appear, but rather with the intention of keeping it completely for themselves, as if they had lawfully taken it.

It should be noted that it is rare to know the owner, unless he sends his agents to buy back the goods in his name. This is the case, first, because the goods are so extremely diverse that we cannot know what belonged to whom and, next, because sometimes up to three hundred persons or more have a share in those commodities. For usually very many people take part in these kinds of sea passages. Consequently, if goods were to be divided into so many parts, each person would get a very small share. Hence, owners do not care to recover the goods. Finally, many do not want it to be known that they incurred a loss, and they hide themselves as much as possible, especially when they have no hope of recovering anything, except at a very high cost.

3. Refutation

As to the first argument in 136, the analogy between a robber and the seller of someone else's goods must be denied. For what the robber sells, he sells against the owner's will, because the owner wants the good to be restored to himself, or, if the latter is not possible, at least to the poor. Yet, in this case, apart from the vendor's inequitable desire to sell the good, there is no unwillingness on the part of the owner, and he has no reason to be against the purchase that we discussed.

As to the second argument in 136, namely that ownership cannot be transferred through such a sale because the seller cannot transfer a right that he does not possess himself, the transfer of ownership onto the buyer does not happen by the authority and will of the robber, but through tacit consent of the owner, who benefits from this kind of transfer. For the ownership is transferred with the burden of restitution in case the owner appears. It could even be said that ownership is transferred under *ius gentium* just as ownerless property, albeit with the burden in the event the owner appears. This is especially the case when the buyer does not foment or partake in unlawful attacks and pillages. For it is in the common interest of the state that uncertain goods do not remain vacant. Nor is it necessary that restitution happens in favor of the poor when goods are bought with chiefly such an intention. Yet we should make sure that they give to the poor to the extent they have been enriched, because that amount should be given back to the owner after subtracting the value of industry and expenses.[6]

As to the third argument in 136, those who buy goods in the aforementioned way, especially in the circumstances that I related, are not accessories to a crime and do not support the main authors in their wrongdoing, since there would absolutely be no shortage of other buyers willing to buy without any intention of making restitution.[7]

6. See above, chapter 14, questions 6 and 7.

7. I have explicitly taken this view from Molina, *De iustitia et iure*, tom. 2, disput. 118, § *Illud Postremo*.

Question 19

Can Someone Keep the Excess Profit if He Has Been Given Something to Sell but Sells It at a Higher Price than He Was Instructed?

138. It is not possible to retain part of the price when he receives a wage for his labor, when he is a servant, or when he has taken on this salesman's task for free. The reason is that he has no legal title to claim a piece of the price for himself—not on grounds of the good sold, because it does not belong to him, or on grounds of his labor or service, because he receives a wage in return. Also, if he was a servant, he was obliged to sell the good without receiving any wage in return.[1] There is no problem if the owner determined the price at which the good has to be sold, because he only seems to have done that lest it be sold cheaper, but not lest it be sold dearer, if the occasion may present itself. This is why even the amount that surpasses the price completely belongs to the owner.

139. Note, however, that if such a servant bought the good from the owner at the indicated price and sold it later at a higher price in his own name, he would do nothing wrong and he would

1. Silvester, *Silvestrina summa*, part. 1, s.v. *Emptio*, quaest. 24 (on the basis of Archidiaconus), and others.

not be obliged to restore anything. For he bought it from the owner at a just price, and he sold it later at a just price in his own name. However, if perhaps the owner had ordered him to sell at any possible price within the bounds of the just price, he has to show that diligence and if so, he would have the right to buy the good for himself from his master at the price the others offered for it.

Question 20

When a Good Is Sold as a Whole to Two Persons Consecutively, to Whom Is It Owed?

Covarruvias treats of this question in his *Variae resolutiones*.[1] I will answer it briefly.

1. When No Delivery Has Taken Place

140. It is common doctrine that the good is owed to the first buyer when no delivery has taken place yet. The reason is that the good could not be sold to the second buyer, because it had already been sold. So there can be no delivery without the first buyer being harmed. Hence, so that no harm would be done, it has to be delivered to the first buyer.

2. When Delivered to the Second Buyer

2.1. Principle

If it has only been sold to the first buyer, but already delivered to the second buyer, it is owed to the second one. This is also common doctrine and is clear from Codex 3.32.15 and Codex

1. Covarruvias, *Variarum resolutionum*, lib. 2, cap. 19.

2.3.20.[2] The reason is that ownership is not transferred by virtue of the contract alone without any delivery, nor does one acquire any right over a good without delivery—with a few exceptions. As is clear from the laws in Justinian's Code just cited, delivery is a prerequisite in addition to a contract.[3]

Applies to many contracts—This does not only hold true for contracts of sale, but also for promises, donations, and similar contracts, even for leases.[4] For even though the delivery of the thing leased does not grant the lessee any title of ownership, he does have detention of the good. If he were deprived of the detention of that good, he would first of all be entitled to restitution by a judge, just as one who has been deprived of a possession. Consequently, he will be able to defend himself by virtue of his right of detention against the first lessee, who only has a personal action against the lessor. Moreover, it does not matter if the contract may have been concluded with the first lessee under oath. Although this does make the lessor commit perjury when he delivers to someone else, it does not hinder the transfer of ownership.[5]

2.2. Exceptions

2.2.1. When Ownership Is Transferred by Virtue of Agreement Alone

141. First, the rule does not hold true in cases where specific legislation allows for transfer of ownership solely by virtue of a contract, without delivery, when something is sold or donated to churches, pious places, or cities in accordance with the provision in Justinian's Code.[6] For in that case ownership is transferred by

---

2. As teaches Covarruvias, in the work above, num. 1; Cod. 3.32.15 (in the beginning and at the end); Cod. 2.3.20.

3. On this, see chapter 3, question 3.

4. Covarruvias, in the work cited above, num. 8.

5. Covarruvias, *Epitome de sponsalibus*, part. 1, cap. 5 num. 9.

6. Cod. 1.2.19.

virtue of the contract alone, so no second buyer or donee will be able to acquire ownership through delivery. It is different when a good has only been promised, because a promise to a place or to someone does not transfer ownership or any real right over the good. Consequently, when you promise a good to the church but donate and deliver it to a third party, it will belong to the latter.

2.2.2. When the Good Is Mortgaged to the First Buyer

Second, the rule does not hold true when the good has been mortgaged to the first buyer as security for the contract. Then, the second buyer will not be able to gain ownership through delivery.[7] The reason is that the person who holds security has to be preferred to a chirographic creditor, especially with regard to that secured good.

2.2.3. When the Second Buyer Acted in Bad Faith

142. Third, the rule does not apply when the second buyer acted in bad faith (i.e., if the second buyer was aware of the first contract, then the first buyer can recover the good as if he had been fraudulently deprived of it).[8] The second buyer is not obliged, however, to spontaneously hand over the good to the first buyer, unless he induced the first buyer to sell it to him, in which case he unjustly causes the damage incurred by the first buyer as a result of the second sale.[9] If, on the other hand, the second buyer was not aware of the first contract, the good cannot be taken from him, unless the first buyer has a title of purchase or another onerous contract, while the second has only a title of donation. In the event the good was donated to the second one, the first buyer will be able to recover the good from the second party even if the latter was unaware of the first

---

7. Covarruvias, in the work cited above, num. 7, on the basis of Dig. 20.5.7 and 13.

8. So reads the commonly accepted Gloss to *Liber Sextus* 3.4.17.

9. In accordance with what has been said in chapter 20, question 19.

contract.[10] Nevertheless, the donee is not obliged to hand over the good spontaneously, but only in the event the buyer claims it within the period laid down by law.[11]

3. When It Is Uncertain Who Was Delivered to First

143. When both buyers affirm that the good has been delivered to them and it cannot be determined who was delivered to first, the good has to be assigned to the first buyer. The reason is that once delivery plays no part, the right of the first buyer is the stronger. Accordingly, when in doubt, favor the first buyer, unless perhaps the second buyer has already paid the price, while the first has not, in which case we assume that delivery has been made to the second.[12]

---

10. As the doctors glean from Cod. 7.75.5. See Covarruvias, in the work cited above, num. 5.

11. In accordance with what I said in chapter 20, question 19.

12. So reads Covarruvias, in the work above, num. 6, based on Baldus and others.

Question 21

Are All Kinds of Monopoly Unjust?

144. It should be noted that a monopoly properly speaking is any effort made by one or a few merchants to ensure that they alone can sell a particular product at a price arbitrarily determined by themselves. In a wider sense, the doctors consider monopoly to be machination and industry deployed by merchants to ensure that they alone can either sell a particular good or decide over its price.

Four types of monopoly—A monopoly can be established in four different ways. Sellers conspire about the price to ensure that no one sells at a lower price, or they make sure that they alone sell a particular good. The latter can be brought about either through a special privilege from a prince, or through industry—namely, by buying up all the goods and then holding them back until prices rise—or through impeding other merchants from importing the goods from somewhere else.

1. A Conspiracy about the Price

1.1. Within the Limits of the Just Price

145. Sellers conspiring about the price are not sinning against justice (but still against charity), as long as the price does not exceed the legal price or the highest common price. The same applies to buyers conspiring about the lowest price or telling other people not to buy a good at a certain price. Now and then this occurs at public auctions when one buyer tells another not to bid higher so that he can buy the good at a lower price. However, to go under the lowest just price of that particular market is not allowed.

146. Note, however, that if some merchants impede others from selling at a lower price through fraud and threats, they are obliged to make restitution to the buyers who suffered damage as a consequence.[1]

1.2. Above the Legal Price

147. If the price stemming from conspiracy exceeds the legal or upper common price, the sellers sin against justice. Consequently, they are obliged to make restitution of the surplus the buyers were forced to pay and of all the damage that ensued from it. The reason is that the price does not depend on the arbitrary will of the merchants. A price should be based on the assessment of a superior or a common estimation made in good faith and uninfluenced by conspiracy or deceit, and of circumstances such as the abundance and scarcity of goods, buyers, and sellers. Therefore, if a person by his counsel or consent causes another person to pay more than this price, then the former is the unjust cause of loss to the latter and so is obliged to make restitution. Note that the person who received the money is obliged in the first place. In second place, that is, in subsidiary order, the other

1. See above, chapter 12, question 18.

conspirators are obliged. They are obliged to make restitution in proportion to their share in the conspiracy.[2]

1.3. Conspiracy by the Buyers

Similarly, buyers who conspire or tell others to underbid the just price are sinning against justice. The reason is that the sellers have a right to a higher price, notably to a price corresponding to an estimation made in good faith. Consequently, the sellers suffer injury from such a conspiracy.

2. A Privilege from the Prince

148. The second mode of establishing a monopoly is when a merchant obtains a special privilege from a prince that lends him the exclusive right to import and sell specific kinds of commodities. In this case a distinction should be made. For the privilege is either based on a just title or it is not.

2.1. Based on a Just Title

If the privilege is based on a just title, then the monopoly is licit too, as long as the just price (estimated by the prince or by prudent people taking into account all relevant market circumstances) is not exceeded. This is notably the case when the prince observes that without the temporary benefit of a privilege no one would be prepared to import a particular kind of good in sufficiently large quantities because of the costs involved. The prince might also decide to sell a privilege if he urgently needs money to be spent for the common good.

149. Note, however, that when the prince grants a privilege for the importation and sale of goods that are essential to the preservation of the political community, he is obliged to fix the price of the goods. If he leaves the price-fixing to the arbitrary will of those who received the privilege, the privilege will be

2. According to what we have said in chapter 13, question 4.

inequitable in this respect. For he gives them the opportunity to sell the goods at an inequitable price to the noticeable detriment of the community—something he in particular is obliged to prevent by virtue of his office.[3] This is not the case with privileges involving luxury goods or products bought for the pleasure that can be derived from possessing them. Nobody is forced to buy paintings, for instance, or special kinds of tapestry, or textile and garments made of silk, let alone dice, packs of cards, game pieces, and the like. Apart from a few rich people perhaps, nobody is obliged to buy these goods. People do not buy these goods, unless they want them out of their own will. Therefore, the prince can easily have a just reason not to impede the goods from exceeding the just price.

2.2. Not Based on a Just Title

If the privilege was granted without a just title, it is inequitable. Then injustice is done both to other citizens who want to sell but are unrightfully impeded and to the buyers who could have got a better price. Consequently, the following persons are obliged to make restitution: first, the sellers who received the unlawful privilege (they are the main cause of the harm done, because they persuaded the prince to grant the privilege and to unrightfully impede others from entering the market); second, those who granted the privilege, at least when it is abundantly clear that the privilege is inequitable. In case of doubt the latter group is not obliged, since the authority and prudence of the prince makes the privilege granted by him get the benefit of the doubt.

3. A Few People Buying Up the Whole Supply

150. The third mode of establishing a monopoly is by buying up all the goods of a certain kind (e.g., grain before, during, or after harvesttime) in order to sell them afterward at a price fixed freely by their own will.

---

3. See the correct remark by Navarrus, *Manuale*, cap. 23, num. 92.

3.1. The Opinion of the Doctors

Several doctors contend that these people sin against justice and are obliged to make restitution.[4] The reasons they put forward are twofold. First, these sellers are doing injustice to the political community by holding back the goods and inducing scarcity. For as long as the supply is stored on its territory, the political community has a right that prevents the price from rising. Second, they commit injustice by afterward selling the goods at a very high price, for this price is actually unjust in their respect, since it is they who, through fraud, are the cause of that high price. This opinion is very probable.

3.2. The Other View is Not Improbable

151. However probable the former opinion may be, the contrary view has never seemed to me to be improbable. It can be argued indeed that such people are not obliged to make restitution as a matter of strict justice, and have not sinned against the principles of particular justice but only against charity and legal justice or public utility.[5] It can be proven as follows.

By buying they have not sinned against justice, for I assume they bought at the current price. Nor is it relevant that, in so doing, they have induced scarcity and high prices, because a large number of buyers also cause prices to rise, and yet they do not for that reason sin against justice by buying, given that the action giving rise to the price increase is not against justice. Nor did they sin against justice by holding back the supply—namely, by not selling—because justice did not oblige them to sell at a time when they had actually not obliged themselves by

4. See Gabriel Biel, *Collectorium circa quattuor libros Sententiarum*, lib. 4, part. 2, dist. 15, quaest. 10, art. 5, dubit. 2; Ioannes Medina, *De poenitentia, restitutione, et contractibus*, tom. 2, cap. *De rebus restituendis*, quaest. 36; and other doctors.

5. This standpoint was already adopted by Molina, *De iustitia et iure*, tom. 2, disput. 345, num. 7–10.

an agreement to do so. They could have held back the goods for another occasion or taken them off to another place or even destroyed them without inflicting injustice on anybody, because they had the absolute ownership over those goods. The members of the community also had no right as a matter of justice to buy the goods if the sellers had not wanted to sell them. Otherwise one would have to conclude that they were going to sin against justice if they threw their wares into the river. Nor is it relevant that the magistrate can force the sellers to bring out their stock and sell at a good price, or that he provides severe punishments for holding back a stock. There are many crimes that can be punished by public authority yet at the same time do not run counter to particular justice, for it suffices that they are in some way against the common good.

3.3. Refutation of the Opinion of the Doctors

152. First, the political community does not have, as a matter of justice, a right implying that the price does not rise if the supply of goods in the city is held back or unknown.[6] For the price depends on the common estimation. Otherwise people selling dear in good faith at that moment would afterward be obliged to make restitution. Consequently, even with respect to those who withheld the supply, the price is not unjust, since they obtained that price without committing any unjust act. The second counterargument only proves that they have sinned against particular justice if the estimation of the price, which takes into consideration the circumstances prevailing at the moment of the sale-purchase agreement, is unreasonable, as when they conspire about the price.[7] That is the way this argument should be understood.

6. This is clear from question 5 above.

7. See above, number 147.

4. Hindering Other Importers

153. The fourth mode of establishing a monopoly is when a merchant applies violence or fraud to prevent more goods from being imported from elsewhere and to keep up the scarcity in the community. In that case he is obliged to make restitution to the political community to the extent that it has been unjustly forced to pay high prices, and to the merchants excluded from the market to the extent that they were deprived from a probable profit.[8] If, however, the merchant has not used any violence or fraud, he is not obliged to make restitution. A survey of the means of punishment for monopolies before the external court is included in Silvester's *Summa*.[9]

8. Silvester, *Silvestrina summa*, part. 1, s.v. *emptio*, quaest. 13.

9. Silvester, *Silvestrina summa*, part. 1, s.v. *emptio*, quaest. 13 and 18.

Book 2, Chapter 28

On Suretyship, Insurance, Pledge, and Mortgage*

* These contracts are in a way accessory to the other contracts, because they are all entered into in order to confirm other contracts or to save goods or obligations running a risk. Accordingly, we rightly have to touch upon these contracts last.

Question 1

Suretyship: Definition and Conditions

1. Definition

1. *Suretyship* means taking on someone else's obligation, thus binding yourself to fulfill the obligation when the principal debtor defaults.[1] It is a verbal contract under civil law because it does not give rise to an action in the external court without the use of the *stipulatio* formula. Without the *stipulatio*, it is as though it were merely a naked agreement.[2] However, under canon law and in the internal court, the formula of the *stipulatio* is not required, since consent expressed in words suffices.[3]

2. Required Conditions

Usually, there are four conditions to this contract that determine its nature.

---

1. See Gomezius, *Commentaria variaeque resolutiones iuris civilis, communis, et regii*, tom. 2, cap. 13, num. 11.

2. As can be gleaned from Cod. 8.40.12.

3. According to what I said in chapter 17, question 4.

2.1. Accessory Obligation

2. The first condition is that the contract should be accessory (i.e., it is assumed that there is or will be another principal debtor or obligation).[4] This is why he is called *surety*, because he "ensures" the fulfillment of another's contract, act, or debt, making himself responsible for the other. It makes no difference whether the surety precedes or follows the principal debt, because someone can stand surety for future contracts of a friend. Likewise, it makes no difference whether the principal obligation arises out of contract, delict, or a court's decision, nor does it matter whether the obligation is both civil and natural or merely natural. For the surety can assume responsibility for all these obligations.[5]

3. It follows that the person assuming the role of principal debtor in favor of another is strictly speaking no surety, because he does not bind himself accessorily or in case of default, but as someone liable on an equal footing. He can therefore be sued immediately.

2.2. The Surety Cannot Exceed the Principal's Obligation

4. The second condition is that the surety cannot make himself responsible for more than what is owed by the principal debtor (i.e., that he fulfills the obligation to a greater extent in another time or place).[6]

Note, however, that the surety can be obliged more strictly, for example, by an oath, by a mortgage, or by a notarial deed (which is called a *guarantigium*), with which the creditor can

4. Inst. 1.4.1 and 3.

5. Inst. 1.4.1; Gomezius, *Commentaria variaeque resolutiones iuris civilis, communis, et regii*, tom. 2, cap. 13, num. 1.

6. Inst. 1.4.6; Gomezius, in the work cited, num. 1. It is common doctrine.

seek immediate foreclosure, even if the principal debtor is not obliged in this manner.[7]

2.3. When the Principal Obligation Is Void

2.3.1. Principle

The third condition relates to the obligation's validity. If the principal debtor's obligation is completely void, the surety's obligation will be void as well,[8] as, for example, when you stand surety for the payment of usury or the payment of the price promised for a sacred good sold by a layman.

2.3.2. Natural Obligation

6. Note that when a natural obligation arises from a contract or some act of the principal debtor for which the surety assumes responsibility, the latter is not only responsible under civil law as the principal is, but also under natural law. The surety can be sued on the very grounds of the principal's failure or unwillingness to perform.[9] This is the case when someone stands surety for a slave, for a minor contracting without the permission of his caretaker, for a cleric entering into a contract without the permission of his superior, or for a woman contracting without the permission of her husband. For these people are only obliged to fulfill the contract to the best of their abilities. So if they call upon a surety, he will be obliged, even if they discharge the obligation by the remedy of restitution into the former legal position or if the persons with the power of ratification render the contract invalid.

7. However, if a minor sells immovable property or movable property of great value without the court's permission and he calls

7. As is shown by Gomezius in the work cited, num. 2, aside from being self-evident.

8. Dig. 46.1.46.

9. As Gomezius teaches in the work cited, num. 2, and as can be gleaned from Inst. 1.4.1.

upon a surety, this surety is not obliged, because this contract gives rise to neither a civil nor a natural obligation.[10] This also applies when a minor buys something for more or sells something for less than half of the just price without the permission of his caretaker, because there is no natural or civil obligation to fulfill that contract.[11]

It should be noted that when there is nothing that goes against justice, and if a surety is appealed to for the sake of the security of the contract, namely, so that it cannot be rescinded by a superior or a remedy, the surety will still be obliged, even if the principal is not. For the surety has made himself responsible for the principal in case the latter is not willing to stick to the agreement. It is different, however, when the surety has only assumed responsibility to pay a debt. In that case, the surety will not be obliged if the contract is legally void, because he has only assumed responsibility in the event that the principal owed something and did not pay.

2.4. After Excussion of the Principal

2.4.1. Principle

8. The fourth condition is that the surety can only be sued if, after excussion of the principal debtor, it has been established that he is insolvent, according to the *Authentica*.[12] Before Justinian's new legislation, one used to be able to sue the surety before excussion of the principal, except in case of a so-called indemnifying surety.[13] For it often happens that the creditor has taken on one or several sureties and still does not feel sufficiently protected, because he does not know whether they have enough goods. This is why he asks someone to in turn stand surety for the sureties. This person is called an indemnifying surety,

10. Cod. 2.23.2.

11. As can be gleaned from the cited law *Secunda* (Cod. 4.44.2).

12. Auth. *Praesente*, Cod. 8.40.

13. Gomezius, in the work cited, num. 15.

because he promises that the creditor will not incur any loss on account of the other sureties, binding himself in the event that they are found insufficient. By its nature this type of suretyship demands the excussion of all prior sureties, which common suretyship does not.[14]

2.4.2. Cases Where Preliminary Excussion Is Not Required

9. It should be noted that there are some cases in which the common surety can be sued prior to the excussion of the principal. First, he can be sued when the surety has renounced the benefit of excussion, which he can do because it exists solely in his favor. Second, he can be sued when it is certain that the principal is insolvent or is somewhere far away and he does not have any goods in this territory. Third, he can be sued prior to the excussion of the principal when he is brought to court and denies being a surety, because in doing so the surety loses the benefit of excussion.[15]

Others add that the surety can also be sued before any excussion of the principal debtor when he has confirmed his suretyship under oath. But as Gomezius rightly points out, this is not true, because an oath has to be interpreted in accordance with the nature of the contract, and it cannot extend beyond the scope the contracting parties or the law gives to the simple nature of the contract he confirms. Therefore, if someone intends to stand surety in the common manner, he can oppose the exception of preliminary excussion. If, however, he had intended to stand surety precisely in the event the principal would be unwilling to fulfill his obligation, and fulfillment could not be obtained from him in an amicable way (as happens when someone stands surety for a very powerful debtor), then the surety would be liable prior to excussion.[16]

---

14. Auth. *Praesente.*

15. Dig. 46.1.10.1.

16. *Dec. Greg.* 2.24.9.

2.4.3. *Ignorance*

If in any of the cases in which excussion is required the surety did not raise this remedy, because he did not know about this privilege, and for that reason he was sentenced to pay, or he already paid, the payment is valid. The creditor is not obliged to make restitution, because such an exception is not induced by law against the obligation and the substance of the claim, but only by reason of the order of procedure. The surety therefore has to raise the exception of excussion before the contestation of suit, because it is a dilatory exception.[17]

---

17. As Gomezius teaches in the work cited, num. 14.

QUESTION 2

WHO CAN ACT AS A SURETY AND WHO CANNOT?

11. All those who can bind themselves as a principal can bind themselves as a surety unless some law forbids it. The main difficulty concerns women and minors.

1. Women

1.1. Surety for Her Husband

12. If a woman stands surety for her husband, the suretyship is invalid by virtue of the *S. C. Velleianum.*[1] So it follows that, if she discharges the obligation on behalf of her husband on grounds of this suretyship, the creditor is obliged to make restitution, because she paid what she did not owe. She did therefore not transfer ownership, since there was no title. If, on the other hand, she made a promise under oath, she is obliged, because you have to keep your oath, unless its execution is harmful to salvation.[2]

1. Auth. *Si qua mulier,* Cod. 4.29.
2. *Liber Sextus* 1.18.2.

1.2. Solemnity Requirements

13. If a woman stands surety without a notarial deed, or with one but without three witnesses, the suretyship is invalid. Accordingly, she is not obliged to discharge the obligation, so the creditor is obliged to restore what she already paid, unless she confirmed her obligation under oath.[3] In the previous two cases, there is no need for the remedy under *S. C. Velleianum*, because the contract is invalid on its own.

1.3. Remedy by S. C. Velleianum

14. If a woman stands surety with a notarial deed and three witnesses, she is obliged as a matter of both civil and natural law, but she still has the remedy under *S. C. Velleianum* in order to repel the creditor's claim. The cited legal provision states the first part explicitly, and it also requires the signatures of the three witnesses on the notarial deed. But it has become established practice that it is enough that a public notary signs the deed in the presence of three witnesses. The other part is to be found in other provisions under the *S. C. Velleianum* and is the common opinion of the doctors.[4]

15. Note, however, that when a woman wants to avail herself of the remedy under this decree of the Roman senate, she repels any obligation so radically that she is not even obliged in the internal court. If she ignorantly discharges the obligation, the payment is valid and the creditor is not obliged to make restitution spontaneously, but when she later realizes she has this privilege, she can avail herself of this exception and claim back what she paid by virtue of the remedy against undue payment. For this exception works in her favor and is certainly not limited to a certain period of time.[5] Consequently, the creditor

3. Cod. 4.29.23, final paragraph. Moreover, it is common doctrine.

4. Cod. 4.29.1, etc., and it is common doctrine, as Gomezius teaches in num. 16.

5. As Gomezius teaches.

will have to pay her back. In fact, the woman can avail herself of this exception, even after a final judgment ordering her to pay, as long as she does it before the judgment is executed. I add this final note because there is no claiming back after a definitive judgment is executed.[6] In that case, the creditor is not obliged to make restitution, because she no longer has any right to claim back, since she waited too long. She can, however, avail herself of the exception after execution if the execution did not happen by virtue of a definitive judgment, but by virtue of a *guarantigium* document that she conceded to the creditor.[7]

1.4. Cases in which She Cannot Avail Herself of the Velleian Remedy

16. First, she cannot avail herself of the remedy if she explicitly renounced it. For anyone can renounce what has been established in their own favor. But a simple renunciation in a deed does not suffice (for a woman can be made to renounce her privileges with the same ease as she is brought to stand surety, so a simple renunciation would not count).[8] For the renunciation of the privilege to be valid, it has to happen in the presence of a magistrate. Whenever a person's age or frailty is the reason behind a privilege, simple renunciation is not sufficient. Renunciation must happen in the presence of a magistrate or under oath, otherwise the privilege would become useless.

17. Second, she cannot avail herself of the remedy when she confirmed her suretyship under oath, because in that case she is obliged to fulfill her obligations even if she did not know of her privilege when she swore the oath. Covarruvias, however, along with many others, thinks that she could avail herself of the Velleian privilege in this case because an oath does not extend

6. Dig. 12.6.59.

7. Gomezius, see above.

8. As clearly shown in Gomezius, *Commentaria variaeque resolutiones iuris civilis, communis, et regii*, tom. 2, cap. 13, num. 17.

to the things that are unknown.[9] Yet the contrary opinion is the common one, as Gomezius says. The reason is that even if she had known of the privilege, she would have still sworn an oath. For she swore the oath with the exact intention of making it impossible for herself to break her promise in any way, so she also implicitly renounced this privilege. I have to admit, however, that Covarruvias' view is probable and safe in practice.[10] Moreover, the other opinion is not that widespread, because many others also exhibit this view.

Third, she cannot avail herself of the remedy if she received a price for her suretyship. For other cases of less weight, see Silvester and Molina.[11]

2. Minors

18. When a minor, someone under the age of 25, stands surety, it gives rise to at least a natural obligation. Nevertheless, he can repel the obligation by the remedy granting him restitution into the former legal position, because he is always presumed to be harmed.[12] However, if a minor stands surety for his incarcerated father, he is effectually obliged. The reason is that he is obliged to do so, otherwise he could be disinherited if he is a male of at least 18 years old.[13]

---

9. Covarruvias, *In Cap. Quamvis pactum*, part. 2, par. 3, num. 5.

10. As taught by Thomas Sanchez, *De matrimonio*, lib 4, disput. 9, num. 15.

11. Silvester, *Summa*, part. 1, s.v. *Fideiussor*, num. 2; and Molina, *De iustitia et iure*, tom. 2, disput. 540.

12. As can be gleaned from Dig. 4.4.7.3; it also is common doctrine, as shown by Gomezius, *Commentaria variaeque resolutiones iuris civilis, communis, et regii*, tom. 2, cap. 13, num. 19.

13. The doctors glean this from Auth. *Si captivi*, Cod. 1.3 and from other laws.

3. Bishops and Clerics

19. As to bishops and clerics, even though they cannot stand surety to the detriment of the church, they can at their own expense, which is established practice. This rule is not hindered by the canon law provision stating that "a cleric who devotes himself to suretyship is removed from office,"[14] because it deals with clerics who devote themselves to suretyship, probably driven by the prospect of profit. Still, the cleric is only liable by virtue of his suretyship to the extent that he is able to carry that load with his patrimony or his benefice's proceeds, provided that he is not left to remain in a state of indigence.[15]

4. Members of Religious Orders

20. Members of religious orders cannot stand surety or accept a loan without the consent of their superior and the majority of the cathedral chapter. Otherwise the religious community is not responsible, except to the extent that the activity was turned to the community's advantage.[16] The same goes for the superior who acts without the consent of the majority of the cathedral chapter, unless it relates to petty matters, which he can dispose of on his own.[17]

---

14. *Dec. Greg.* 3.22.1.
15. *Dec. Greg.* 3.23.3.
16. *Dec. Greg.* 3.22.4.
17. Silvester, *Summa*, part. 1, s.v. *Fideiussor.* num 4.

Question 3

Can Each Surety Be Liable for the Whole Debt?

1. Response

21. First, when there are multiple sureties securing the same debt, every surety is liable for the whole debt.

***Remedy against* in solidum *liability*—**Yet, the one sued for the entire debt can make use of a remedy so that any given surety can only be sued for his share of the debt. For instance, three sureties assume responsibility for the payment of 300 guilders. If the debtor defaults in paying and one of the sureties is sued by the creditor, he can only be obliged to pay 100 guilders. This surety can then ask the creditor to go and collect the rest of the debt from the other sureties.[1] This privilege has been granted to them by a rescript from emperor Hadrian, where the same is stated. Without this remedy, every single surety would be liable for the whole debt under the contract of suretyship.

1. So Dig. 46.1.26 and Cod. 8.40.3.

22. Second, this remedy has to be introduced prior to the definitive judgment ordering to pay.[2] After that judgment—especially if that judgment commissioned execution and the payment has been made—the remedy cannot be introduced, according to what I said earlier related to women. If the surety was forced to pay not by virtue of a definitive ruling, but by virtue of a *guarantigium* deed, then he can still exercise his remedy.[3] The same goes when the surety appeals against the definitive judgment.

23. Third, the surety has no right to the remedy if he has already paid, either of his own accord or by force of a definitive judgment. This is also the case when he renounced this privilege when entering into the contract.[4] This remedy is therefore weaker than the privilege a woman has, because she can reclaim what she paid under *S. C. Velleianum* if she has paid without knowledge of her privilege.

2. Remark: If He Paid the Whole Debt

The surety who has paid the entire debt can compel the creditor to assign to him his personal claim against the other sureties, namely, the creditor's claim to demand the other sureties' share in the debt, which he could have demanded from every single one of them under Hadrian's rescript (e.g., 100 guilders from each surety in my example). In addition, this surety can claim back from the principal debtor his own share in the debt, that is, 100 guilders. This way he will be able to recuperate the 300 guilders he paid. The other sureties, however, can only claim back their share from the principal. Furthermore, the surety who paid for the principal and in doing so incurred damage, can claim from the debtor not only everything he paid, but also compensation for the damages incurred on the debtor's account.

---

2. As taught by Gomezius, *Commentaria variaeque resolutiones iuris civilis, communis, et regii*, tom. 2, cap. 13, num. 15.

3. Gomezius, in the same place.

4. Gomezius, see above.

Question 4

Definition of *Insurance*. Requirements for the Insurance Contract to Be Just

1. Definition and Requirements

1.1. Insurance

24. *Insurance* is the coverage of another's risk, that is, it is a contract in which someone takes on the risk of another's good, obligating himself either for free or at a certain price to indemnify the other party if the good is lost. If he takes on this obligation for free, it is a gratuitous promise. If he takes on the obligation for a certain price, it is a contract similar to a sale-purchase agreement. For the one who insures goods for a price seems to put up for sale his obligation to pay the value of the goods in case of loss, while the other party seems to buy this obligation.

1.2. Equality

For the insurance contract to be just there has to be an equal balance between the price paid to the insurer and the obligation he takes on, namely, in such a way that the obligation is worth as much as the price that is given for it according to the judgment of a knowledgeable man. For just as in a contract of sale where there has to be an equal balance between the price and the good for sale, here there has to be an equal balance between the price and the obligation sold to the other party.

2. Consequences

2.1. When You Know the Goods Are Safe

The insurer cannot collect premiums when he knows for sure that the good has reached its destination prior to the contract (e.g., it has reached the port, the journey to which he insures), because the obligation he takes on has no price, since the condition under which he obligates himself (namely, if the good should perish before it reaches the port) is completely impossible, and he knows that for sure. This is confirmed by the fact that he does not expose himself to any potential risk. Indeed, the obligation that the insurer takes on cannot be priced except on the basis of some possible risk. Consequently, the insurer cannot ask a price. In this case, therefore, the contract is void, first, because a good is sold that has no price or value and, second, because fraud gives rise to the contract. So it also follows that the insurer is not only obliged to make restitution of the price he received, but also to compensate the contractual expenses and damages incurred.

If, however, the insurer did not know for sure that the goods were at their destination, he could demand the price corresponding to the estimation of the value of the risk he subjected himself to. The higher the risk is thought to be, the higher the price that can be asked, and vice versa, even if in reality there is not any risk. For a risk is considered to be worth as much as it is estimated to be in good faith.

2.2. When a Merchant Knows His Good Has Been Lost

25. If a merchant who wants to insure his good knows with certainty that this good has been lost, he cannot enter into a contract to insure it. Nor can he demand to be repaid its value. The reason behind this is that the obligation he is claiming is an obligation to something that he himself knows is impossible. For it is impossible to cover the risk of a good when it has already been lost, because coverage and insurance against a risk presume that the good is still subject to the risk, or that it at least possibly is. If, however, one knows that the good has been lost, then one knows it cannot be subject to any risk and, accordingly, that it cannot be insured. Moreover, it cannot be insured because fraud gives rise to the contract. For the merchant deceives the insurer by indicating that the good, which he knows to have been lost and still seeks to insure, has not been lost, or that at least he thinks it has not been lost yet. Therefore, if the insurer compensates the value of the good that has been lost, the merchant is obliged to pay him back that value. On top of that he is obliged to cover the damage that may be the result of that contract. The insurer, on the other hand, is obliged to refund the collected premium, because the contract was void.

26. However, if it was not fully certain whether the good had been lost, it seems that the merchant can still demand something from the insurer.[1] For by paying the premium, the merchant exposes himself to the risk of losing that premium without any disadvantage for the insurer, because when the good happens to be safe, the insurer keeps the premium without any harm. So if the good does perish, the merchant is able to claim something more than the premium from the insurer, because if the latter can make a profit, then equity demands that he can also lose. But he cannot lose, unless the merchant can demand something more from him than the collected premiums. In conclusion, he will be able to claim the amount he would have offered himself, had he known the truth about the good, or at least the amount that should have been offered in such a situation, according to the estimation of a prudent man, considering all circumstances.

1. As Molina remarks in *De iustitia et iure*, tom. 2, disput. 507.

2.3. When One Insurer, in Particular, Knows That There Will Not Be Any Risk

27. Note that if a lot of money (e.g., 3 percent) is regularly offered to cover large risks, which are mostly caused by a storm or pirates, whereas I, in particular, know beforehand thanks to astronomical information or some other source that there will not be a storm, or if I know thanks to a friend's letter that there will not be any pirates or that the company will not run any risk, then I can nonetheless collect the common insurance premiums. For the obligation is generally estimated to be worth as much as it is because the risks that commonly occur are large. In fact, hidden causes that lower the risk, and that only I know of, do not lower the common estimation, because the general public is unaware of them. Just as commodities can be sold at the price that they are generally estimated to be worth by professionals—even though that estimation is contingent on their externally perceived rarity and does not correspond to reality because there still are in fact many goods that are hidden or about to enter the market—so too can this obligation to insure be sold at the price that it is commonly estimated to be worth by professionals, even though that estimation is contingent on the common opinion about risks, which you know can be lowered here and now.

3. Questions and Answers

3.1. When the Insured Goods Are Fictitious

28. Suppose someone does not have any commodities on his ship, but he feigns that he has goods up to a value of 10,000 guilders that he wants to insure for 500 guilders for the journey from Antwerp to Spain. When his ship subsequently perishes, is the insurer obliged to pay 10,000?

I answer briefly that if, on the one hand, the insurer knew or suspected that there were no commodities or that they were not worth that much, he is obliged to pay, because it is considered to be a betting contract.[2] That is, if the ship arrives at the port unharmed, the insurer makes a profit of 500; if it perishes, he loses 10,000. If, on the other hand, he thought in good faith that the commodities did exist or that they were worth that much, we have to make a distinction. If he entered into the contract with the intention of contracting even if he had known that there were no goods, he is obliged to pay, since there was tacit consent to bind himself even in that situation and consequently to expose himself to risk and profit. If, however, he was not intending on entering into the contract if he had known this, for fear of fraud or for any other reason, then he is not obliged. Yet, he is still obliged to pay back the premiums as soon as he finds out about the fictitious nature of the insured goods, since he did not consent to the contract.

29. ***Determination of the commodities' value***—Yet usually insurers do not really care about the intrinsic value of a good, but only about its estimated value. If there are any commodities, this estimated value has to be applied proportionately. So if the entire shipment is lost, the entire value has to be paid, even if the goods were estimated far above the just price. If half of the shipment perishes, half of the estimated value has to be paid; if a third perishes, a third is to be paid, and so on.

3.2. When There Are Several Insurers

What happens when there are several insurers who have each agreed to bet on a part of the loss, and half of the commodities are lost?

30. I respond that, if each share is specified, the insurers are only obliged to the extent of their share. If the shares are not specified, every insurer is obliged on a pro rata basis of the total amount of lost goods. For instance, if the commodities are

2. As Sotus rightly points out, *De iustitia et iure*, lib. 6, quaest. 7, art. 1.

estimated to be worth 8000 guilders and there are four insurers who each cover a fourth of the total loss (i.e., 2000 guilders), when half of the shipment is lost, every insurer is obliged to reimburse 1000; when a fourth is lost, they reimburse 500, and so on.

Question 5

Pledge and Mortgage

31. Note that a pledge is properly speaking the thing that is delivered to the creditor, while a mortgage is merely contingent on a contract, without the need for delivery.[1] The name *pledge* (*pignus*) stems from the word *fist* (*pugnus*), because it is delivered from hand to hand (in Greek, ἐνέχυρον). This is why a pledge is properly speaking a moveable good, whereas a mortgage is an immovable good. Yet this distinction is not completely carried through, because the terms are often used as synonyms in legal texts.[2]

32. ***In a wider sense the terms are used in three ways***—First of all, they are used to denote the thing itself. This way, the terms *pledge* and *mortgage* are used to denote goods that are moveable or immoveable, material or immaterial, which the debtor and creditor agree to hold as security for a debt, so that when the debtor defaults, the creditor can obtain payment by selling the goods. Second, the term *pledge* also stands for the contract or

1. Inst. 4.6, § *Item Serviana*.

2. As shown by Inst., as cited above.

agreement under which the pledge is established. Third, *pledge* also denotes the obligation that arises from the real contract. In a similar way the terms *loan for consumption*, *loan for use*, and *deposit* are used for the goods themselves, the contracts, and the obligations arising from the contracts.

Question 6

In How Many Ways Can a Mortgage Be Established?

Generally speaking, one enters into a contract of mortgage in one of two ways: explicitly or tacitly.

1. An Explicit Mortgage

33. One can contract explicitly in two ways: by agreement of the parties or by judicial decree. First, one can contract by agreement of the parties. This is called a conventional mortgage, which only requires the parties' consent, without the good's presence or delivery.[1] Second, one can contract by judicial decree. This is called a praetorian pledge, which requires that a judge or magistrate transfer possession or detention of a good to a person.[2] Some distinguish between a judicial pledge and a praetorian pledge, but there is no need for that.[3]

---

1. As is made clear by Dig. 20.1.1. For more on this, see Negusantius, *Tractatus de pignoribus et hypothecis*, part. 3, membr. 1.

2. As is made clear by Dig. 13.7.26.

3. As can be gleaned from Cod. 8.21.1–2, where every kind of pledge established by a judge is called praetorian, whether it is established before

2. A Tacit Mortgage

34. The contract is entered into tacitly when it is established by a legal norm. In fact, this is often the case in the Roman law tradition:[4]

1. When one owes to the treasury or the prince on account of a contract or taxes, all his goods are tacitly mortgaged in the latter's favor.[5] An exception is made for a minor who buys something from the treasury, in which case only the good bought is mortgaged for its price. If, however, your goods are confiscated as a direct result of a crime, they are not considered to be mortgaged, but as being owed to the treasury if you are sentenced later.[6]
2. **35.** The entire property of a husband is mortgaged as security for his wife's dowry. The same goes for the property of the sureties if the husband has called upon them to stand surety for giving back the dowry. These mortgages and the treasury are given priority over other tacit mortgages prior to them in time, yet not endowed with a similar privilege. They do not, however, take priority over prior explicit mortgages.[7]

---

or after a definitive judgment. The same can be gathered from Dig. 13.7.26. See Negusantius, *Tractatus de pignoribus et hypothecis*, part. 3, membro 2.

4. These cases are mentioned by Silvester, *Summa*, part. 2, s.v. *Pignus*, quaest. 2; and Molina, *De iustitia et iure*, tom. 2, disput. 526; and very elaborately by Antonius Negusantius, *Tractatus de pignoribus et hypothecis*, part. 2, membro 4. Most of what follows is based on the latter.

5. Negusantius, *Tractatus de pignoribus et hypothecis*, part. 2, membro 4, num. 113.

6. Negusantius, at the place cited, num. 115.

7. As I said in chapter 15, question 4; Negusantius, at the place cited, num. 108.

3. When you promised a dowry, all your property stays mortgaged until you fulfill that promise.
4. A minor is granted a mortgage over the property of his guardian or caretaker for the administration of his property.[8]
5. The church is granted a mortgage over the property of prelates and ecclesiastical administrators for the administration of its property, because it enjoys the same benefit as a minor and ward.[9]
6. The city is granted a mortgage over the property of city administrators for the administration of its property, because it enjoys the same benefit as a ward.[10]
7. A son is granted a tacit mortgage over the property of his father when the father manages that son's property.[11]
8. The entire property of the deceased is mortgaged for the legates.[12]
9. If a husband donates something to his wife or it is donated on his behalf, and the husband dies, it belongs to the shared children. If the woman then remarries, all her goods acquired after that donation are mortgaged as security for the donation to the benefit of the shared children. The same holds true when something is donated by a wife or on her behalf to the husband.[13]
10. **36.** Everything bought with a ward's money stays mortgaged for the price to the ward's benefit. The ward has

8. Negusantius, at the place cited, num. 6.
9. Negusantius, at the place cited, num. 120.
10. Negusantius, at the place cited, num. 119.
11. Negusantius, at the place cited, num. 13.
12. Negusantius, at the place cited, num. 157.
13. Negusantius, at the place cited, num. 20 and 22.

a preferential right to payment above all others who have a mortgage over that good. The same goes for everything bought with a soldier's money.[14]

11. The landowner is granted a mortgage over the proceeds of leased goods for the rent.

12. Everything added to a leased estate has to be repaid to the landowner for the rent and for the damages incurred by the leased good, whether it is located in town or on the countryside. However, if the estate is located on the countryside, all adaptations have to be executed while the owner is in full knowledge of it, otherwise they are not obliged.[15]

13. When money is given on loan to rebuild or restore a building, that building is mortgaged for the amount of money lent. The creditor is given preferential right over all other prior and even explicit mortgages established on the same building. The only exception to this is the wife's mortgage for her dowry, which takes priority if it was established first.[16]

14. When money is lent in order to build, buy, or decorate a ship or to provide it with necessary equipment, that ship is mortgaged for the amount of money lent, just as is the case with the house.[17]

15. **37.** When money is given on loan to preserve goods, these goods are mortgaged for the amount of money lent. Moreover, the creditor has preferential right to payment over other, prior mortgages. (Examples include: when someone gives money in order to repair a ship or

14. Negusantius, at the place cited, num. 163–164.
15. Negusantius, at the place cited, num. 128 and following.
16. Negusantius, at the place cited, num. 162.
17. Negusantius, at the place cited, num. 162

a building, to procure the sailors necessary to maintain the ship, to transport the commodities, or to hire a security force to accompany the commodities, and so forth.)[18]

Some of these instances are not prevailing law everywhere, and laws and customs differ from province to province. For instance, in some places under a contract of sale all property of contracting parties is perpetually and legally subjected to a special mortgage, so that no extinctive prescription liberates the debtors. This custom is of course very different from Roman law.

3. Universal and Particular Mortgage

38. Both types of mortgage—tacit and explicit—in turn come in two variants: universal or particular. A universal mortgage affects all property. This should not only be understood in terms of present property, but also of future property that the debtor will acquire within a certain period of time.[19] This does not, however, prevent goods from being sold freely, because the price acts as their substitute. A particular mortgage affects a certain thing. It always affects the good, to whomever it may belong, until what is due is paid, the obligation is acquitted, or it is extinguished by prescription.

18. For more, see Molina, *De iustitia et iure*, tom. 2, disp. 438 and 536; Antonius Negusantius, *Tractatus de pignoribus et hypothecis*.

19. As is made clear by Cod. 8.16.9.

QUESTION 7

WHAT CAN BE GIVEN AS PLEDGE?

1. Things That Cannot Be Pledged

1.1. Right of Patronage

39. What cannot be sold cannot be pledged (e.g., a church, cemetery, or a grave).[1] A right of patronage can therefore not be pledged.[2] The reason being that it is not a thing that could compensate a pecuniary debt. So even if a castle or a farm connected with a right of patronage were to be pledged, the right itself would not be considered to be pledged and the first patron would maintain his right of presentation. However, if the good with which the right is connected is sold, the right is transferred to the buyer along with it, as well as the right of presentation, because the accessory follows the principal.

1. Dig. 20.3.1.2.
2. *Dec. Greg.* 2.27.18.

1.2. Goods of the Church

Immoveable goods and precious moveable goods dedicated to divine worship, such as chalices or chasubles cannot be the object of a pledge, unless it is necessary and handled with due solemnity. It is possible, for example, when debts cannot be paid otherwise, or when prisoners belonging to the church can be freed or the hungry fed, because in these and similar cases the goods can also be sold.[3] These goods can, however, be the object of a universal mortgage.[4]

1.3. A Freeman

40. A freeman cannot be the object of a pledge.[5] When you are made captive, however, you can hand yourself over as a pledge for the price that someone else paid on his own behalf until the price is paid back in money or services. Yet, a freeman can be given as a hostage, especially in wartime, so that agreements are met. In case of noncompliance by the state or prince who handed over the hostage through no fault of said hostage, he cannot be killed on that account (according to Exodus 23: "thou shalt not put to death the innocent and just person"), nor can he be mutilated or whipped, because these measures cannot be taken absent any offense. They can, however, deprive him of his property, detain, and enslave him, if he is not a Christian, just as all other innocent people in times of war.[6]

1.4. A Surety in a Criminal Case

41. Things are similar when someone stands surety for an accused who faces capital punishment or mutilation, so that

---

3. See above, chapter 24, question 10.

4. As can be gleaned from *Dec. Greg.* 3.13.5. See Silvester, *Summa*, part. 2, s.v. *Pignus*, num. 3.

5. As is made clear by *Dec. Greg.* 3.21.2.

6. For more, see Thomas, *Summa Theologiae*, 2a2ae, quaest. 40, art. 1, dub. 7.

he can temporarily be released from prison. When the accused escapes through no fault of the surety, the latter cannot be punished by execution, mutilation, or whipping in his stead, because these are criminal penalties, not a liberation from debts. The surety did not intend on binding himself to make sure the accused does not escape, but only to pay the pecuniary punishment the judge sentenced him to. Moreover, the surety could not even take on such an obligation, because he is not lord over life and limbs.[7]

2. All Other Goods Can Be Pledged

42. All other goods can be the object of a pledge, as long as they are given by persons who freely manage them, irrespective of whether the goods are moveable or immoveable and material or immaterial (such as annuities, debts, taxes, and even jurisdiction, because it is often considered to be worth quite a lot).

3. Remarks

3.1. Fruits Pledged Accessorily

43. If you pledge a field or some other fruit-bearing thing, the fruits you have sown or that sprouted at that time are pledged and also stay pledged, even if you sell the good in the meantime and the buyer collects the fruits.[8] However, fruits sown or sprouted after an alienation or a lease are not pledged, with the exception of the period during which they are still hanging or are connected to the soil. Such fruits are the object of the pledge because they are considered to be one with the soil, so the creditor can claim those fruits if he deems fit, but after subtracting the expenses the buyer or lessee made in cultivating them.[9] When the fruits are separated and gathered they stop being a pledge,

7. This is common doctrine, as is indicated by Iulius Clarus, *Sententiae receptae*, lib. 5 (*Practica criminalis*), quaest. 46, num. 18, final paragraph.

8. As is made clear by Cod. 8.14.3 and Dig. 20.4.11.3.

9. Dig. 20.1.16.3.

unless they are collected by an heir who is entitled to that thing through inheritance.[10]

3.2. A Pledge Can Be Pledged

44. A creditor who has taken a pledge from a debtor can in turn give that thing as a pledge to his own creditor.[11] The reason that he can transfer the right he has on that pledge as a pledge to another is that rights and claims can be the object of a pledge. However, once the creditor has received payment of the debt, the second pledge is terminated because the first pledge on which it was based has been terminated as well.

3.3. Extinction of the Pledge

When ownership of the pledge or mortgage is transferred to the creditor in whose favor they were pledged, the hypothecary claim he had against the previous possessor is extinguished, because he has become possessor himself (unless you would like to say that he has a claim against himself). The same holds true when the creditor destroys or extinguishes the mortgage himself. For example, if the right of payment under an annuity contract that A has over B's farm is given as a pledge to B, and B extinguishes it or buys it back after having paid back the sum to A or to C, who had bought the right from A, then the hypothecary claim is also extinguished along with the mortgage itself. You cannot say that the sum has replaced the mortgage as when a price replaces a sold good because real obligations are transferred and extinguished along with the goods. Real obligations do not hop from one good to another unless explicitly agreed upon. This is clear in the case of a sale of a mortgaged house because even if it is only sold to be destroyed, the price does not remain due. This is supported by the fact that hypothecary obligations

10. Dig. 20.1.29.1. See Molina, *De iustitia et iure*, tom. 2, disput. 529, and Silvester, *Summa*, s.v. *Pignus*, num. 2–3.

11. As is made clear by Cod. 8.23.1–2.

are cumbersome and disagreeable and must accordingly be restricted to what has been expressly agreed upon. Therefore, when someone's annual property income is mortgaged in plain wording, it is not in any way to encompass the price of the annuity. It is no problem that, when the income is subject to a fideicommissum, the price for which it is bought back is subject to the fideicommissum as well. For the income does not belong to the heir burdened with the fideicommissum in absolute terms, so neither does the price. The heir only has a kind of usufruct and he is obliged to give back those goods in perfect condition to the person awarded with the fideicommissum.

More could be said about this matter, but it can either be gathered easily from the above-mentioned authors, or it pertains to the external court, where laws and customs are extremely diverse in different provinces.

About the Contributors

Jordan J. Ballor (Dr. theol., University of Zurich; PhD, Calvin Theological Seminary) is a research fellow at the Acton Institute for the Study of Religion & Liberty and serves as executive editor of the *Journal of Markets & Morality*. He is also the author of *Covenant, Causality, and Law: A Study in the Theology of Wolfgang Musculus* (Vandenhoeck & Ruprecht, 2012) and *Ecumenical Babel: Confusing Economic Ideology and the Church's Social Witness* (Christian's Library Press, 2010).

Wim Decock (PhD, University of Leuven and Roma Tre) is research professor at the Faculty of Law, University of Leuven, and an associate researcher at the Max Planck Institute for European Legal History, Frankfurt am Main. He is the author of *Theologians and Contract Law: The Moral Transformation of the* Ius Commune *(ca. 1500–1650)* (Nijhoff/Brill, 2013).

Nicholas De Sutter obtained his BA in law and MA in Latin and English linguistics and literature from the University of Leuven in 2015.

Stephen J. Grabill (PhD, Calvin Theological Seminary) serves as senior research scholar in theology and director of programs at the Acton Institute for the Study of Religion & Liberty. He is editor emeritus of the *Journal of Markets & Morality*, as well as author of *Rediscovering the Natural Law in Reformed Theological Ethics* (Eerdmans, 2006) and editor of *Sourcebook in Late-Scholastic Monetary Theory* (Lexington, 2007).

Sources in Early Modern Economics, Ethics, and Law

Jordan J. Ballor and Stephen J. Grabill, General Editors

Books in This Series

A Treatise on the Alteration of Money
Juan de Mariana
Translated by Patrick T. Brannan • Annotations by Stephen J. Grabill
Introduction by Alejandro A. Chafuen

On the Law in General
Girolamo Zanchi
Translated by Jeffrey J. Veenstra • Introduction by Stephen J. Grabill

On Law and Power
Johannes Althusius
Translated by Jeffrey J. Veenstra • Introductions by Stephen J. Grabill and John Witte Jr.

On Exchange and Usury
Thomas Cajetan
Translated by Patrick T. Brannan • Introduction by Raymond de Roover

On Righteousness, Oaths, and Usury
Wolfgang Musculus
Translated by Todd M. Rester • Introduction by Jordan J. Ballor

On Exchange
Martín de Azpilcueta
Translated by Jeannine Emery • Introduction by Rodrigo Muñoz

A Treatise on Money
Luis de Molina
Translated by Jeannine Emery • Introduction by Rudolf Schuessler

The Mosaic Polity
Franciscus Junius
Translated by Todd M. Rester • Edited by Andrew M. McGinnis

Of the Law of Nature
Matthew Hale
Edited by David S. Sytsma

On Sale, Securities, and Insurance
Leonardus Lessius
Translated by Wim Decock and Nicholas De Sutter • Introduction by Wim Decock

Made in the USA
Monee, IL
14 September 2026

62974529R00125